BELIEVE

A Journey of Enlightenment

By

Deborah Fields

ISBN:0615468993
ISBN 13 -9780615468990

This book is dedicated to the memory of my amazing parents who now reside among the stars.

To my partner and husband, Vincent DiClemente, whose unwavering belief in me allowed me the courage to spread my wings and fly...

And to all of the Lightbearers, who are walking their paths to spiritual enlightenment and are in the process, illuminating the way for all to follow.

"There are only two lasting bequests we can hope to give our children, one is roots; the other wings."

-Hodding Carter-

Contents

Magical Prayer

From beneath me arises the energy of the earth; my home and my foundation.

From above me pours the light of the Sun and the enchanting Moon.

To my right hand flows the strength to control and direct the power of magic.

To my left hand comes the skill to divine and to heal, the source of blessing.

Unknown

Source: Magical School

INTRODUCTION

For me this has been a journey of love and light, of understanding and enlightenment and of empowerment of spirit. This journey all began for me years ago as I tried to understand the meaning of life. Why were we here? What was our purpose?

While in college I began to read everything I could get my hands on regarding metaphysics and quantum physics. As I studied there were truths I embraced and others I discarded; not because the truths I was studying were incorrect. They were simply not right for me at the time. In many ways I had to grow into these truths or more importantly when the message was right for me to hear, I embraced it. Or more correctly it embraced me. I encourage you to do the same. Only embrace what resonates within you as truth. You do not necessarily have to be a student of metaphysics or even a religious person to begin to understand spirituality and the concept of spiritual evolution.

You may be drawn to the information within the pages of this book because you are looking for answers that will clarify the meaning of life for you or you may be on your own personal quest and have come looking for guidance. You may be experiencing a shift in the parameters of your reality and want to move to the next level of your spiritual evolution or you may be reading this book simply out of curiosity. Whatever your reasons are for reading this book, the principles and tools given within the pages of "Believe" can help and assist you along the road in your own personal journey and expansion of spirit.

The parameters of my own personal journey have been defined and held within an ever changing and shifting matrix that has been evolving for me throughout my lifetime. The pathway along this journey took a sharp turn for me in 1986 when my parameters and boundaries shifted in what was a life altering experience. I was having troubles within my marriage that later ended in divorce and was having a very nice pity party for one! I was sitting on my bed and meditating on what the purpose of my life was and why I was in this current situation. As I meditated I suddenly felt myself tumbling backwards and in that moment for me, time seemed to stand still .It seemed like an eternity before I stopped tumbling and landed on my feet. As I looked around I was aware of being in a very unfamiliar place. I remember glancing around in total confusion and wondering what in the world had just happened to me, and where was I? As I began to focus on what was around me I saw that I was standing in front of a very long hallway and at the end of this hallway was a door that was slightly ajar filled with a brilliant white light. As I stared in shock, the door opened up and Christ was standing in the doorway with his arms outstretched towards me. A wave of unconditional love hit me and permeated my being and with this wave, thoughts flowed through me telling me that everything would be alright and that I was walking my correct path. The voice told me I was protected and for me to believe and to not lose faith. With this, an overwhelming fear come from? Seven years later I finally began to listen to the voices that were urging me to open up to channel. It was then that I started the process of recording what later became the manuscript "Believe". It took me seven years to finally be comfortable with this awe inspiring gift and there is not a day that goes by that I don't offer up to the divine realm a sense of gratitude for what has been given to me. Through this process of listening, or more correctly a process where ideas, thoughts and information stream through my mind on a much higher frequency, I began recording what I was hearing. This is called automatic writing. After my seven-year hiatus, on June 17, 2008, I sat down finally and opened up to channel and a crystal clear voice commanded me to be still and listen! This process, as a very dear friend has described it, is like having coffee with a friend. It is a process where after meditation, giving thanks and invoking protection, I sit down at a table or desk with pen and paper and open up to a higher frequency that is definitely not my own. When you open to channel, a very specific higher frequency that oscillates on a continuum in the ever expanding ethers at all times, moves through your mind and fills you with light and divine energy. This is an amazing experience wherein an indescribable sense of peace and unconditional love moves through your body and fills your being with total awe and wonder.

This collaboration is between myself and the divine beings who are speaking through me. During this process I can interrupt and ask questions at any time to clarify what it is I am hearing.

Sometimes in the middle of a session I'll read what I just wrote and be floored by the information I just received. At those times when I stop to question, a very gentle voice admonishes me to step aside and to just let the process happen, to let the thoughts flow uninterrupted.

I knew immediately that I was receiving wisdom from a much wiser source than myself. When I questioned whom it was that was speaking to me, a very clear voice told me I was receiving knowledge and wisdom from the Divine Principals on the other side of the veil. The voice told me "we speak to you as one voice of peace and enlightenment, of knowledge and wisdom and are tapping into the ever present, ever constant flow of the universal mind of God". We are the archangels and the ascended Masters of the Great White Brotherhood. What you are receiving is divinely inspired and guided. You wonder who to give credit to as to the Divine Principals who are speaking to you? We are known on this side of the veil as Mother Mary, Jesus the Cosmic Ascended Christ who has been your guide throughout all lifetimes, Saint Germain who has been with you always, Melchizedek who has guided you throughout all of time and beyond, Omri Tos who has been your guide and mentor throughout many incarnations, the Archangels Uriel, Michael, Raphael and Gabriel who are always by your side and guide, protect and direct you constantly, the Archangels Zadkiel and Metatron who come in as needed and Lord Arcturus who is now at this moment in time instrumental in guiding and directing your spiritual evolution as well as the information being imparted to share with all who choose to read. You are to have faith in the process. You are to accept this, embrace it and share this information with others. You must do this with gratitude, unconditional love and acceptance in the knowledge that we are with you always and it is our voice that directs the course of this book and all ones to follow. You were given many blessings at birth and writing will combine all of these gifts into one cohesive package that will enable you to reach many with your consistent message of hope, love and enlightenment for all. This is your destiny. Embrace it, accept it and get on with it. You have procrastinated long enough!" Quite frankly I was speechless, floored and overwhelmed by what I had just heard! My immediate thought was, "Well, I guess they just told me"! In many ways what they did was give me a good swift kick in the butt and admonished me to get moving.

I was told these divine truths and principles are being given to humanity to use at this crucial time in our history. These divine truths are no longer just for the Adepts and Avatars of the ages but are now being made available for all to use. They are now available to all who have both an open mind and a desire to learn, understand and comprehend. These truths and principles will bring about illumination and enlightenment. To all who embrace them, they can set them free. They are being given now very much as a wake-up call; A call to be alert and to pay attention to the messages given.

Time is of the essence. We need to all remember who we are. The calendar for the illumination of mankind is no longer measured in eons but is now being measured in years. It is now at this moment in time and space imperative that you honor not only yourself but also the world that you live in. My guides have said "We will illuminate all who embrace these words of wisdom to the secrets of the ages." They told me the messages revealed within this book and all the books to follow were important teachings that have all been hiding in plain sight where most knowledge is most often hidden.

We all need to believe in something, even if that belief is the belief in nothing! We need to believe in something bigger than ourselves in order to feel secure in the world around us. Whatever your beliefs are, they give you a solid foundation and open the door to your spirituality or lack thereof.

Each of us has within us the ability to see, hear and sense the other side. There are moments in time when all of us sense a greater power other than our own. We all have moments of clarity when the unexplainable happens to us and we are each given a glimpse of another reality that exists just beyond our five senses. Haven't you ever been thinking about someone and the phone rings and that person is on the other end of the line? Maybe you were thinking about a question you needed answers to and the answers came to you through the program you were currently watching or through the radio you were listening to, at just the right moment.

When that happens a light bulb goes off in your head and you realize that what you just heard was exactly what you were searching for! Sometimes a perfect stranger will come up to you and tell you exactly what it is you need to hear, coincidence or divine help? I'll leave that for you to decide.

Each tool and principle contained within this book can not only help you achieve inner peace and harmony but can also help guide you along the yellow brick road towards your own spiritual enlightenment. Every prayer given within the pages of "believe" provides you with the necessary tools that can assist in awakening the power of god that dwells within you as you. Every chapter gives you hope and a pathway to follow. The tools and principles of love and light are available to all who choose to embrace them. They impart clarification, joy, wisdom, trust and unconditional love to all in a wave of tremendous energy and blessing from the divine realm.

So I give to you these words of wisdom in the hope they inspire you as they have me. Embrace what resonates within you as truth and disregard what does not. Take the journey into self that is offered within these pages and find your own light of illumination.

"Together let us watch in wonder the magic of the morning sun shining through a green leaf."

-Laura Teresa Marquez-

Early Morning Conversation

CHAPTER 1

THE BALANCING OF LIFE

"Solitude in the sense of being often alone is essential to any depth of meditation or of character; and solitude in the presence of natural beauty and grandeur is the cradle of thought and aspirations which are not only good for the individual, but which society could ill do without."

- John S. Mill -

The balancing of life is truly one of the most challenging occupations we can aspire to. It is a constant challenge to keep our Four Body systems in perfect harmony. These four bodies are comprised of our physical, emotional, mental and etheric bodies. The physical body is the composition of our gross anatomy and behind the obvious physical being that we all acknowledge lays a series of more subtle vehicles of consciousness comprised of our mental, emotional and etheric bodies. These three more subtle bodies could collectively be called our psyche. The psyche is not a single entity in the way our physical body is but rather the sum total of our very distinct subtle bodies which are in essence vehicles of consciousness that exist as frequency levels within the spiritual plane of existence. When in balance all four bodies vibrate in unison to a single frequency and energy flow. This frequency flows throughout the various channels, nadis, or meridians as pure undiluted energy. Our nadis or meridians comprise our energy matrix that is composed of the sum total of all four bodies and is the channel through which this energy then flows throughout our bodies to achieve perfect harmony and balance. This energy is then processed within our energy centers or chakras.

Within the subtle anatomy our emotional body correlates to our wants, desires and to our emotional feelings. Our mental body is the instrument of reason, imagination and thinking. Our etheric body is our blueprint for our physical body and is the subtle life force that sustains the life of the physical body. This life force is often called our ch'i or prana, which is identified with the breath of life and is the life force of the soul. These three subtle bodies are innate in everyone and upon the death of the physical body are converted into a higher frequency. This frequency then becomes our spiritual body and it is this body, which houses our soul that we carry with us for all eternity.

Our physical body grounds us to the earth and is connected to all of nature. Our emotional body processes all of our wants, desires and needs. Our mental body is the vehicle through which we manifest our realities and our etheric body is our direct connection to whatever our concept of God is and to our own divinity. It is this last body that houses our spirit or soul. It is through this body that in sleep we are able to transcend out of the physical body and travel back home to the realm of the divine. This process is called astral travel or is often referred to as an 'out of body' experience. It is vitally important to our total wellbeing. It is through this process we experience déjà vu. When we leave the physical body at night so our soul or spirit can stretch its legs, we have a total freedom of being and can move both laterally and vertically in time therefore moving through past, present and future simultaneously.

We as human beings need this freedom of being which nourishes the soul in the same manner that food and water nourish the body. Without this freedom of being we would never be able to tolerate the confinement of the physical body. When all four bodies are in perfect sync and harmony, our connection to what I will often refer to as the divine realm, is assured. The divine realm has also been referred to as Heaven, the other side of the veil, Summerland, Shangri La, Nirvana and the next dimension just to name a few. All of these descriptions are correct depending upon your belief system and point of view. It is this connection to the divine realm that keeps us all centered and balanced.

We are all beings comprised of total energy and vibration that lives in every cell, atom and nucleus of the body. Within all of us exists energy centers each vibrating to a different frequency of color and sound. These energy centers directly control the different systems and organs within the human body and are also directly linked to our four body systems total well being.

We all have within us seven energy centers that align us from within. These energy centers are centers of light that are anchored within the etheric body which then governs the flow of energy to our four body systems. These energy centers are called chakras. The concept of chakras was borrowed from the Vedic tradition of India and was known and used in ancient Egypt and Tibet. Sanskrit calls a chakra a wheel or a circle. The American Heritage Dictionary states that a chakra is one of seven centers of spiritual energy in the human body according to yoga philosophy. Essentially a chakra is a wheel of spinning energy. There are seven wheels of spinning energy that reside within us all. The cultures of Asia have been implementing the wisdom of healing from within by aligning these seven wheels of spinning energy for centuries. These wheels govern both our gross anatomy as well as our subtle anatomy and are directly linked to our four body systems. The total exchange of energy between the matrix of our four bodies and the matrix of our chakras is vital to our very existence.

This chakra system is located just in front of your spinal column and is aligned vertically up and down your spine. When these spinning wheels of energy are in perfect harmony, optimum energy flows freely throughout your entire body and you can then achieve a complete wellness of being. Adepts throughout the ages have been successfully employing these techniques to heal the entire body. When these seven wheels of spinning energy are in perfect balance and harmony they connect us to the divine realm and to God. They connect us to the seven seats of consciousness and to the seven Elohim of creation who are the seven powers of God, which I will explain more fully in the next chapter.

Within each of our chakras there exists a seat of consciousness represented by all the emotions that are held there. Each of these chakras vibrates to one of the seven colors in a color spectrum represented by the rainbow, as well as to each of the seven vibratory notes held within a musical scale .Also the seven Elohim of creation are each represented within the seven chakras within the human body. When you employ the visualization techniques described within this chapter you can bring your entire body into balance in a matter of minutes. Through this technique you then have the tools at your disposal on how to reduce pain within the body which in turn helps to accelerate the healing process. In so doing it is then possible to make a quantum leap of faith by believing in these principles and applying them within your own body to create a total wellness of being.

To balance your chakras, you mentally visualize the color of that particular chakra vibrating within the area of the body that it governs. You visualize this color pulsating within that energy center and then in turn pulsating throughout your entire body. You feel your entire body radiating with this color. You then feel the area of the body governed by this particular chakra coming into balance, which then in turn balances the area of the body that it correlates to. You use this technique for each of the seven chakras until your body is in perfect harmony and balance. You breathe into it. You become one with it. You might visualize each chakra having a scale within it that when in perfect balance then brings complete alignment to that area of the body that it governs. Once this is achieved you might feel a tingling occur throughout your body. This is normal. This tingling is the quickening of the energy within your body and is the quickening of your own personal spiritual vibration. It is this quickening from within that then brings the body back into balance. By balancing and restoring the energy within the chakras we then bring into harmony all four of our bodies. We do this through meditation, prayer, visualization, and channeling or by simply listening to music or communing with nature. My guides have given me a prayer that you can say that will bring into your presence the divine realm that will then aid and assist you in bringing your chakras as well as your four bodies into perfect balance and harmony. This prayer is as follows:

'I give thanks to the Universal Spirit for providing me with a perfect body through which I can experience life to its fullest.

I ask Spirit to aid and assist me in balancing all seven of my chakras as well as all four of my bodies until all are vibrating in perfect balance and harmony and are now aligned within the light.

I call upon the Divine light of creation to come down through the top of my head and enter my crown chakra like a lightening bolt.

I ask that this Divine light vibrate and oscillate within all seven of my chakras and all four of my bodies until all are totally balanced within the light.

I ask that the Universal Spirit open up each of my chakras until all are now vibrating with unconditional love and compassion bringing me into total alignment with all that is and all that will ever be.

I ask the light of creation to expand each of my chakras and to radiate the color of each chakra throughout my entire body until I am now in synchronistic harmony and balance with the Universe and am now in perfect radiant health and well being.

I do this with an attitude of gratitude that the Universal Spirit has answered my every call.

Thank you Mother- Father God it is done. "

It is also important to denote that illness is often first found in the chakras before it then manifests into the body. A blockage of any one of these chakras creates a problem within all of the other chakras and then pushes them all out of alignment and balance thus creating dis-harmony and a dis-ease of the body.

The following is a description of the function of the seven chakras, what colors and vibratory notes they correspond to, as well as what parts of the physical body they each govern. I will be quoting throughout this description, Shirley MacLaine, from her enlightened DVD entitled "Inner Power". I urge everyone to watch it as it not only explains in a very understandable way what the chakras are and how they function, but it also guides you through both an open-eyed and a closed-eye meditation that teaches you in a very visual way how to balance your chakras and how to reconnect with yourself through meditation.

To prepare for balancing your chakra's, sit or lay down in a comfortable position and breath deeply letting the cares of the day slip away. Now using the technique previously given visualize the colors within each of your chakras that are provided below coming into total balance and harmony, as you do you will bring into balance your entire body and bring about a true wellness of being.

The first chakra is called the root chakra. It is located at the base of your spine about two inches above your tailbone. Many believe it to be located within the uterus in the female and within the scrotum in the male. This chakra resonates to the color red and to the vibratory note of C. When our root chakra is in perfect harmony and in perfect balance our roots are then deeply secured within Mother Earth and she then nourishes and protects us. It is through this chakra that you feel grounded to the earth. All of our fears of flight and fight are centered within this chakra. This chakra has often been referred to as our survival chakra. It controls the function of the adrenals and of the kidneys. It is within this chakra that we have the energy to get up in the morning. When we meditate upon this chakra we release tension in our spine and with it any anxiety that we are harboring.

Our second chakra is referred to as our sacral chakra or our sexual chakra. This chakra resonates to the color orange and to the vibratory note of D. It is located about two inches below the belly button. This chakra governs our personal relationships and our sexual creativity. It controls the fluids within the body; the ovaries in the female and the testicles in the male. It also controls the uragenital systems. When we meditate upon this chakra we release tension within our sexuality and we then realign that sexuality within the balance of the whole.

Our third chakra is referred to as our navel chakra or our solar plexus chakra. This is located at our belly button. This is the energy center of all our personal feelings. It resonates to the color yellow and to the vibratory note of E. This chakra is our clearinghouse for all emotional energy and gives us more problems than any other chakra. It is within this chakra that we carry anger and hate. It controls the spleen, stomach, liver, gallbladder and pancreas. When this chakra is out of harmony and balance a dis-ease then manifests within the different organs governed by this seat of consciousness and we become jaundiced in a true distortion of the color and energy that is held there. When we meditate upon this chakra we are able to release all negative emotion and can then achieve total balance and a true lightness of being.

The fourth chakra is the heart chakra and is located within your heart center. This chakra resonates to the color green and to the vibratory note of F. It is our energy center of love and harmony. It governs the blood, heart and circulatory system. It also has a very strong influence upon the endocrine and immune systems. The Asians say the soul resides within the heart chakra. We feel love through this chakra. This energy center balances the lower three chakras which connect you to mother earth with the upper three chakras that connect you to the divine realm and to God. This chakra is our healing center. It is within this chakra that all of life began. This is where the breath of God, the Holy Spirit, first entered your physical body at first breath and began the heart to beat. At this moment the holy trinity of love, wisdom and will entered your body to reside within your heart and to connect you to your divine self. It is through this chakra that you move upward into your own divinity.

The fifth chakra is referred to as the throat chakra. This chakra is located at the base of your neck. It expresses your wisdom of self-expression, language and communication. It resonates to the color blue and to the vibratory note of G. It controls the thyroid gland and governs the vocal cords, the bronchial apparatus and the alimentary canal. How we interact with the world around us is directly reflected in this chakra. It is our voice which either reflects our divinity or our lack thereof. When this chakra is in perfect balance and harmony we use our voice for the uplifting and enlightenment of all humanity. When we resonate in unconditional love for all we connect with the divine realm through our throat chakra. When this chakra is unbalanced and through our negative emotions becomes warped, it can cause great destruction and will then pollute all of the other chakras. Use it wisely as it is your bridge to the divine.

The sixth chakra is referred to as our third eye or brow chakra. It is located in the middle of your forehead. It resonates to the color indigo and to the vibratory note of A. In some who are more spiritually advanced this chakra will resonate to the color cobalt blue which represents the mind of God, which I will fully explain in the third chapter. It is through this chakra that we manifest our abundance, that whatever we can imagine we can create and in so doing we co-create with God. Through this chakra everything and anything is possible. We daydream through this chakra. We create our realities through this chakra and when it is in perfect balance there is nothing we cannot achieve. When we meditate upon this chakra it can help us resolve grief and it is also very influential with nightmares. This chakra controls the pituitary gland. The mystics have said if you tickle the pituitary you can achieve one unlimited thought. If we dream it, we can do it. There is a saying that Linda Goodman in her book "Star Signs" spoke of. She said, "If you don't mind, it doesn't matter." It is really just that simple. If you don't imagine you cannot create. Believe in yourselves; this chakra is your direct link to all of the abundance you have ever imagined.

The seventh chakra is referred to as your crown chakra. This chakra is located at the top of your head. It resonates to the color violet, or in those who are more spiritually evolved it will resonate in perfect harmony with the violet consuming flame which I will describe more fully in the third chapter, and to the vibratory note of B. This chakra is directly associated with our destiny and our divine purpose. This chakra represents the heart of God. It is through this chakra we link with our true divinity. What is our purpose here on earth? Who are we? This chakra is our direct link to whatever our concept of God is. This chakra controls the pituitary, pineal and the hypothalamus glands. Which are sometimes symbolized by the thousand-fold lotus, and represents the holy trinity within of Mother God-Holy Spirit- Father God. It is through this chakra we can achieve unlimited consciousness and it deals with issues that move beyond language and understanding. Within this chakra are all the counterparts to all the other chakras and when perfectly engaged, connects us to our own divinity and there is then nothing we cannot achieve.

When our seven wheels of spinning energy are in perfect balance, whatever we can imagine we can then create. Whatever we dream then becomes our reality. Imagine just that! Imagine the power this would then unleash when invoked. Then imagine the possibilities that would arise within a world that resonated in perfect harmony. When we are in perfect harmony we bring balance to our world and we bring balance to each other. We then create harmony and balance within our universe and all rejoice.

It is through this harmony of spirit that we can truly change the world we live in to a more abundant world for all. We can change our world to a world of peace, unconditional love and tolerance for all. It is up to each and every one of us to achieve this. When we do we will eradicate all of the disharmony that now exists within our world and bring about a true balance to our universe. We will bring about balance to ourselves and to each other. In so doing we will bring a peace the world has never known to our planet.

Imagine all of the world's governments and people resonating in perfect harmony. Imagine us all uniting as one.

All hope for the future of our planet lies within each and every one of us. Each of us needs to find our balance within and to then reach out and help balance the whole. It is only when we achieve this that we will truly unite as one. This is our birthright. This is what each of us has on some level has been striving to achieve.

The Divine Masters are at hand here and present to offer assistance. All pathways will become illuminated when we invoke their help. All roadways will be cleared of debris. It is up to all of us to help bring about the change that is so needed on this planet. Who will take up the challenge? Who will begin the journey? We all must. All we have to do is believe: to believe in ourselves, to believe in each other and to believe in a higher power that will help us all transcend the boundaries of time and space and bring peace and harmony to our planet.

CHAPTER 2

THE ELOHIM OF CREATION

"What is true is invisible to the eye. It is only with the heart that one can see clearly."

- Antoine de Saint-Exupery -

All of life stems from the divine source. All of life began when the mind and heart of God expanded and in total unconditional love and breath of vision invoked the light. Out of the light came all the rest of creation. In that one single invocation of "let there be light" all of the darkness was dispelled, for light is the true will of God. Where there is light there cannot be darkness. In divine will and invocation all the rest of creation came into being and with it was born the duality of all of life. In the book of Genesis all of creation was created within seven days. These seven days of creation directly correspond to the seven Elohim of creation who are the seven powers of God and to the seven seats of consciousness represented by the seven chakras held within the human body.

The divine light of God is represented within each of our heart chakras by the Holy Trinity of light: by Mother God, Holy Spirit and Father God. Each of these is represented respectively by the living colors pink, gold and cobalt blue. It is this Holy Trinity within that directly connects us to our own divinity and to the love, wisdom and will of the divine realm.

When we meditate or pray and visualize these three colors expanding within our hearts, moving up through our throats and out through our brow chakra and up to the divine realm and to the seven Elohim, the connection is unbelievably powerful. When we pray we bring ourselves into the presence of God. When we do we tap into the same creative power that God used to create the universe. When we achieve this it is then possible to tap into the powers of the seven Elohim of creation. To prepare for prayer breath deeply and let yourself relax, let all of your worries fade away. Visualize in your mind your own personal image or dream of abundance, hope, peace compassion and oneness with all that is. Feel this image or dream wash over you and become one with you .Feel this dream you have visualized move through your body and feel it resonate deeply within your soul. Now visualize yourself connecting to the seven Elohim and to God. When we make this connection and ask God and the Elohim to be in our presence we bring into form the very thing that we desire and then the Universe fulfills our dreams and give us all the abundance that we have ever imagined.

The seven Elohim are all knowing and all encompassing. They are omnipresent and carry within them the highest vibration of the light; a light which we can only truly comprehend in our spiritual evolution of being. They are the seven divine spirits that stand before the throne of God and are aspects of divinity and as such performed the miracles of creation of the universe under the direction of the Holy Trinity. Elohim is a Hebrew word that expresses concepts of divinity. Within the Hebrew grammar it is generally understood to denote the single God of Israel.

In an article from 'Glossario' by Dr. Stone, the description of Elohim is as follows. "The Elohim are the cosmic beings who God created to help Him create the infinite omniverse. The Elohim are more of the mind aspect of God and the Archangels and Angels are more of the feeling tones of God. The Ascended Masters are more the balance between the two. These are the three lines of evolution in God's infinite omniverse."

The Elohim embody the light of the Holy Trinity whom they personify within our seven energy centers or chakras within the human body. They radiate the seven rays of color within the color spectrum and are represented within our seven seats of consciousness. They are the most powerful aspect of the conscious God and are the builders of creation. They are the Alpha and the Omega of the sacred Aum of the "I am that I am'.

The seven mighty Elohim are as follows: The first elohim is "Arcturus", who is known as the acting presence of God. The first Elohim Arcturus has a focus in the Star Arcturus within the constellation of Bootes. Arcturus is one of the brightest stars in the universe. He is associated with divine mercy and righteousness. Arcturus is the greatest of the seven mighty Elohim and is mirror-like as he reflects all the other Elohim within himself. He is also known by many as the almighty healer of the universe. The second Elohim is known as "Cassiopeia" and is the Elohim of wisdom, omniscience, understanding, illumination and the desire to know God. Cassiopeia helps us to know the truth when we see it, feel it, or hear it. He was also known as Apollo in ancient Greek mythology. The third Elohim is known as "Cyclopea", the all Seeing Eye. Cyclopea is the single eye of God who lets us know there is but one source from which everything comes which can never be disconnected and to which we always return. The fourth Elohim is "Purity" and represents purity, hope and the resurrection and ascension process. She is feminine and is depicted as holding the scales of justice in one hand and brandishing the sword of purity in the other. She is the energy that works with and has held in place, along with the divine master Saint Germaine, the violet consuming flame for all of humanity to work with forever, which I will fully explain within the next chapter. The fifth Elohim is the Elohim of "Peace", this Elohim is the breath of God and represents peace and harmony. This Elohim is associated with calmness, grace and tranquility. She is feminine and is associated with the dawn and has often been referred to as the "dawn of Peace". When we experience the breath of God in our silence we experience a peace that has an all understanding and our lives are never again the same. The sixth Elohim is known as "Hercules". Hercules represents the strength of God that allows us to do exactly what needs to be done to bring ourselves back to our own divinity and to a conscious awareness of our true being rather than who we thought we needed to be. The great strength of Hercules originated and is drawn from his obedience and his great love and respect of the will of God. Our modern day Olympic games are directly influenced by this mighty Elohim. During ancient times in the Greek civilization Hercules was seen by all as the supreme athlete. It is due to this collective vision that the Olympic Games were ascribed to him. Hercules was known as the mighty one and was worshiped and held up as a true hero. He was truly the forerunner to all the hero worship that permeates our society today for our modern day athletes. The last and seventh Elohim is "Orion". Orion is the heart of God and is mirrored in the heavens with the three stars of Orion in the constellation. These three stars of Orion are duplicated within each of our heart chakras by the three rays of light of the Holy Trinity which directly connect us to the heart of God, the seven Elohim and to our own divinity. Orion is known as the Elohim of love. He reflects back to each of us our own connection to the divine and our great capacity for unconditional love. Orion is the gateway we must all pass through to connect to the divine realm and to God. He is the gateway to our ascension into our spirituality and is the key to our true spiritual evolution for without embracing unconditional divine love, true ascension of spirit cannot occur.

Divine love comes from and is intertwined with divine will, which emanates from the etheric level of our being and is the closest concept to pure consciousness we will ever have. Divine will, emanates from our inner most being as pure intelligent light. Divine will and divine love can be accessed through prayer, supplication, chant, invocation and meditations in whatever forms you choose.' The Lords Prayer' known by many as the' Our Father' is a perfect example of a prayer that can be said to invoke both divine will and divine love.

This prayer is as follows:

Our Father which art in heaven

Hallowed be thy name.

Thy kingdom come.

Thy will be done, on earth, as it is in heaven.

Give us this day our daily bread.

And forgive us our debts, as we forgive our debtors.

And lead us not into temptation, but deliver us from evil;

For thine is the kingdom, and the power, and the glory.

Of the Father the Son and the Holy Spirit

Forever and ever. Amen."

No matter which of the methods you use to invoke Divine Love and Divine Will, all of them are perfect vehicles for achieving our enlightenment of spirit and of receiving into our beings these two great gifts and remember there are as many ways to pray and meditate as there are people who walk the earth.

Within our spiritual evolution we are now being required by the vibratory changes that are occurring upon our planet to raise our consciousness both individually and collectively out of our self-imposed limitations. We have created these limitations within ourselves due to our forgetfulness of self and due to our turning our backs upon our true spirituality. The only way to raise ourselves out of this limitation of spirit is to transmute all of the negativity back into the light of spiritual evolution, to let go of old and antiquated ideals and to begin to embrace new ideals of unconditional love, peace and harmony for all. Nothing can be changed within our beings or in our worlds until it flows through our consciousness and is then transmuted back into the light.

When we call upon the Elohim, the Ascended Masters, the arch angles and God to come into our lives and to help us eradicate all of the negative baggage we have been carrying around, we are then bathed in light and understanding and we then move into an altered state of consciousness wherein anything and everything is then possible. When we call upon these divine beings we move into them, through them and become one with them and in the process are invoking our own divinity. We are invoking unconditional love, will and wisdom into our lives which when combined is a powerful sword that cuts through the garbage and cleanses the soul. It is the only thing that does and it is the only tool that has the power when invoked to change our world in an instant. To change our world to one of peace where all war, hatred, bigotry, prejudice, rape, incest, child abuse and all crimes against humanity are completely eradicated. I give to you the following prayer to invoke these divine beings into your presence, to empower you and in turn cleanse your soul of all the negative energy you may have been harboring.

"I call upon God, the Elohim of creation, the archangels, and the ascended masters to come into my presence and free me from all of the negative baggage I have embraced in not only this lifetime, but in all other lifetimes as well, both known or unknown.

I ask that you lift me up into the light of compassion, unconditional love and understanding so that my entire being is now completely free of all this negative emotion.

I ask that you move through me and become one with me and in the process I ask that you invoke my own divinity.

I ask that you bestow upon me the divine power to change my world in an instant to love, peace, hope, abundance, compassion, and harmony where all are then transformed into the love and grace of god.

I ask that you help me to remember who I am and assist me in bringing myself back to the true spiritual being I have always been.

I ask that you shine this divine light upon me so that I will then remember what was; embrace what now is; and have the power to co-create and to imagine what will be.

I send this with divine love

Thank you Mother – Father God it is done."

We all need to collectively imagine a better world. We all need to collectively begin to change our own world and begin to let go of the negativity we have been carrying around. We need to imagine how that new world order would be. How would it feel? What would it look like? What constitutes our part in the change that is now occurring? "Imagine all this." Hold that thought and keep it close to your heart. Breathe life into it and begin to create a better reality. The reality we are all currently living in is obviously not working and is crumbling around us. Out of this chaos we all need to begin to rebuild our world. We all need to take part in this manifestation of spirit into reality. We need to extend the olive branch of peace to all we encounter. We need to offer it up to all who will receive it and to collectively recreate harmony, dignity, accountability and everlasting hope in our world and in so doing to bring about a better reality for all.

Believe in yourselves. The power to bring about change is in all of our hands. We are living in an age of intense purification and transition. We are currently witnessing the disintegration and reintegration of the socio-economic matrix of our planet. We all need to be aware of our part in the process of co-creating with the universe and the divine realm. Our own destiny lies in peril. When we all collectively realize that our power in co-creating our realities is truly unlimited, true transformation will occur and the socio-economic matrix of our world will reintegrate before our eyes into a new world order. We need to balance the relationship between our economic reality and our social and mundane realities and merge the three into a true synergy of Spirit. It is in this way that the reintegration of our socio-economic matrix will occur. We have on some level forgotten to embrace and integrate our spirituality with all the other factors and levels that comprise the matrix of our world; from economics to politics, to our relationships with global communities to the media and to the every day social interaction that occurs. We have all forgotten that the very essence of that spirituality defines who we are at any given moment on both a personal level as an individual as well as on a global and universal level as a nation. We need to get back to the beliefs and ethics of our Forefathers who founded this great nation wherein one of the most widely accepted ideas was that a divine hand had established and ruled the nation. Our Forefathers believed an unseen intelligence was the guiding force that directed and defined the course of the American Revolution, which enabled us to move into a reality of freedom and to escape from the tyranny that had previously defined us. Patrick Hendry said, "There is a just God who presides over the destinies of nations". We would all do well to remember that as we move into the new vibratory harmonics of the Aquarian Age.

As we embrace these new vibrations and incorporate them into our lives, we will then begin the journey of visualizing a new world order and true change will then occur all across this beautiful planet. It is within this process that a new reality will begin to materialize which will then transform our world into a world of abundance, hope and prosperity for all mankind. When we embrace the power within and become more than we thought we were, we transcend time and space and unite with all that is. We become one with the universe, with the seven Elohim and with God and the parameters of our world will then redefine themselves. All we have to do is move beyond the boundaries of unlimited consciousness and connect with the universe. It is through this connection we will transcend limitations and embrace the possibility of change for all. All we have to do is believe.

CHAPTER 3

THE LIVING COLORS OF CREATION

"I believe that imagination is stronger than knowledge.

That myth is more potent than history.

I believe that dreams are more powerful than facts.

That hope always triumphs over experience.

That laughter is the only cure for grief.

And I believe that love is stronger than death."

\- Robert Fulghum -

- Storytellers Creed -

In the inception of the Aquarian Age at the dawn of the new millennium in the year 2000, a great shift occurred on our planet. This shift was a shift in consciousness. With this great shift a new vibration was born that ushered in the Age of Aquarius and put to rest the Piscean Age.

Where the Piscean Age was attuned to the vibration of love, the Aquarian Age is attuned to the vibration of light. Love and light are all there is. They are the glue that literally holds the universe together. With this shift of vibration from one age to another came the complete synergy of love into light. Along with this complete synergy two forms of 'living light' were introduced into the world for all of humanity to use. Both of these forms of living light come directly from God and the divine realm.

The first of these living colors is cobalt blue, which comes from the mind of God. The second living color is the violet consuming flame that comes from the heart of God. Both of these when invoked are very powerful tools that can be life altering.

You can use the following two prayers to invoke these two forms of living light into your presence. The first of these prayers comes from the mind of God and resonates to the color cobalt blue.

You invoke, out of the mind of God, the cobalt blue flame by envisioning this color pulsating around you and permeating and oscillating within every cell and atom of your body until you become one with this living color. You can envision this color surrounding your body in a bubble of cobalt blue. When invoked this is the strongest protection prayer you can ever give yourself. This prayer is as follows:

"I call upon the Archangel Michael to come into my presence and ask him to, with his sword, bring out of the mind of God the cobalt blue flame and send it spinning down into my presence like a lightning bolt. I ask him to flash, spiral, spin, enwrap and enfold this cobalt blue flame around my being, my body, my world so that I am now held within the protection of this living color of God and am now invisible, invincible, and invulnerable to anything and everything except the divine protection of God."

You give this prayer the power of the spoken word when you call or invoke it into your presence. At the end of this prayer you simply say, *"I am that I am that I am"*, that invokes the trinity from within and connects you to the divine light of creation. You do this in an attitude of gratitude to the Archangel Michael and God for answering your every call. If you do not want to say "I am that I am that I am" simply say Amen, Amen, Amen.

When this prayer is invoked the protection around you is profound. You can use this prayer to protect anything and everyone in your world. This prayer from the mind of God has the ability to enlighten all who use it. It has the power to trigger within us a remembrance for who we really are: spiritual beings dwelling within the confinement of a mundane world. All of us are spiritual beings on a quest for enlightenment. All of us are walking along this same road. We are just approaching it from different directions. All of our journeys are authentic and all of them are vastly important for the completion and total harmony of the whole. We are all interconnected one to the other and are all unique in our evolution of being.

The second of these prayers comes directly from the heart of God and resonates to the living color of violet represented by the violet consuming flame. The fourth Elohim, Purity, along with Saint Germain, holds this violet consuming flame in place for all of humanity to use forever.

You bring the violet consuming flame into your presence through the power of the spoken word either in prayer or in meditation. You envision the color violet permeating and oscillating in every cell and atom of your body until you are one with the violet consuming flame. You envision this color surrounding your body in a bubble of violet. You call or invoke out of the heart of God the violet consuming flame that is the only power on this planet that can eliminate all human negativity through the following prayer:

"I call upon Saint Germain, the Archangel Michael, the mighty Angel from Venus "Victory", Jesus; the Cosmic Ascended Christ, the Archangel Zadkiel who works only with the violet consuming flame and Omri Tos who is the ruler of the violet planet which is the secret love star of the bible. I ask that these divine beings send the violet consuming flame spinning into my presence until it

permeates through every cell and atom in my body and with this flame to consume and purify all human suffering that I have ever created in any time frame, in any dimension, in any universe both known or unknown. I ask these divine beings to blaze, consume and purify the cause, the effect, the record and the memory of all human negativity that I have ever created within my physical body, my emotional body, my mental body and my etheric body until all four of my bodies are lifted up into the consciousness of love, light, peace and harmony so that I am now truly able to be of service according to divine will for divine purpose according to my divine plan and I am now validated and I am now that violet consuming flame in action here in its most powerful dynamic activity of love, freedom and purification. I am that I am that I am, or you can simply say Amen, Amen, Amen."

When invoked the living light of the violet consuming flame is so powerful. When we call it into our presence and meditate upon it, it expands our consciousness and transmutes our reality into one of total awareness of the divine realm both from within and from without. The violet consuming flame invoked out of the heart of God enters our beings and fills us, illuminates us and cleanses away all of the spiritual debris we have ever created. It cleanses, purifies and expands our consciousness as well as all seven of our chakras and all four of our bodies. When all of these are vibrating in perfect harmony within the violet consuming flame we are then resonating in consciousness within the heart of God. We are then one with the universe and true peace and harmony descend upon us.

Both of these prayers can change your life and protect and transmute your realities into the love and light of creation. They can, when invoked, aid and assist your soul's upliftment and ascension into the synergy of love and light and guide you along your pathway within your own evolution of spirit.

The following is another prayer that you can use to combine both the power of the cobalt blue flame as well as the violet consuming flame and bring them into your presence. It is a prayer I use everyday as soon as I wake up as it not only grounds me but it also protects not only me but also everyone and everything I surround it with. Please feel free to interject into this prayer whatever it is that you want to personally protect. This prayer is as follows:

"In the name of Mother - Father God whose power is greater than any power on earth or in heaven .I ask that my aura, my husbands aura , our home, our property, our business's, our automobiles, our bank accounts , our identities , our investments, our abundance, and the aura of all our family and friends be sealed with triple cones of golden white light .I ask that this golden white light be infused with the cobalt blue flame of protection and the violet consuming flame of transmutation . I ask that everything be surrounded with a mirror like substance so that anything of a negative nature is deflected back to its source. I send it all back with divine love. Thank you Mother-Father God it is done."

You can use any of the two endings that have already been given at the end of this prayer. This particular prayer really works for me however; I encourage you to use whichever one resonates with you. All three are very powerful.

The violet consuming flame is the power and authority upon this planet for the next ten thousand years. It has been given to everyone to purify both themselves as well as all of the negative energy they have been bombarding the planet with. There are thousands of beings working now in this moment of time and space with these two living colors to bring about peace and harmony to our world, to bring about balance once again to our planet. They are collectively helping to negate the negative energies on this planet and transmute them back into the synergy of love and light. There is a spiritual revolution occurring upon our planet whose collective mission is to evolve our world back into the love and light of creation; back into a balance wherein all are connected, all are powerful, all are one.

Each one of these invocations of the living colors of God is ended in "I am that I am that I am". That one phrase is so powerful because it is at the same time both a noun and a verb. You must never put a negative behind it as it is equally as powerful in the negative as it is in the positive. The phrase "I am beautiful" is equally as powerful as the phrase "I am ugly". Each of these phrases will bring into your presence very powerful connotations of both the positive and the negative aspects of both of these emotions. When "I am" is attached to any word it will then invoke strong powers of that word for all words when spoken have the power to either build or to destroy. This is one of the secrets hidden within the spoken language. The following is a prayer or mantra you can use to invoke the power of the "I am that I am that I am" into your life. It is as follows:

"I thank the Universal Spirit of all that is for this day and I choose to see only light, love, and innocence within myself and others.

I invite the presence of that Spirit into every situation.

I choose to be all that I AM and to know that it is safe to honor and cherish my true identity.

I AM a spiritual being in a physical body.

I AM love, loved, loving and lovable.

I AM a beautiful, desirable and empowered person.

I know that true prosperity is perfect health, wealth, and happiness.

I accept that Spirit is the source of all supply and that money is Spirit in action.

Love is flowing from me and to me so richly and so fully that I have abundance, prosperity, and affluence to share and to spare today and always.

My body regenerates itself and I emanate perfect health.

I AM breathing fully and vibrantly today and always.

I choose to give up difficulty and to be a living example of human potential.

These words I speak in faith and they activate a law of Universal good and I accept and share the results.

I AM grateful for these blessings, for the increase in them and for all others knowing that we prosper together in every way.

I AM rich in my heart, I AM rich in my soul, I AM rich in my life, I AM rich and I AM whole.

Thank you for blessing me". (Author unknown)

We need to guard what we speak because when we speak our words simultaneously resonate within our chests, move up through our throats and out through our foreheads as all three are connected. This connection creates the power of the spoken word. When the voice is engaged either for positive or negative it engages the heart, throat and brow chakras and it is within this engagement of voice we can then create our dreams. When we give voice to those dreams, which reside in our hearts and imagine them in our minds, anything and everything is then possible. When we do this we activate our pineal, pituitary and our hypothalamus glands, which collectively represent the Holy Trinity within of Mother God, Father God and Holy Spirit. These three glands work together in harmony in order to bring about a total balance between the human body and our spiritual awareness. The pineal gland is known as the 'seat of illumination', the pituitary is known as the 'seat of the mind' and the hypothalamus is known as the 'seat of the emotions'. Within our physical body the hypothalamus balances and links our nervous system to our endocrine system through the pituitary gland but it is also important within the Holy Trinity in activating the pineal gland and third eye wherein we then perceive through a much higher dimension. When all three of these glands are vibrating in unison we create a powerful magnetic field where anything and everything is then possible. In this complete synergy our personalities represented by the hypothalamus and pituitary glands and our soul represented by the pineal gland, become one. They then collectively activate the light within us. When this is accomplished we can achieve astral projection and our soul can then withdraw from the confinement of the body and fly. Our soul is connected to the body in life by the silver cord of creation. At physical death this silver cord is severed and the soul then withdraws from the body carrying with it the divine light of creation that resides within all of our heart chakras.

You can activate this synergy of spirit through meditation and prayer and in the process open up the third eye through the following prayer:

"I give thanks to the Universal Spirit and feel this Spirit fill my entire body with love, light, and wisdom.

I invoke the power of the holy trinity to activate the light within me so that I Am vibrating in unison with all that is.

I feel the power of this synergy of spirit awaken this magnetic field within me so that I Am now aligned within all the powers of the universe where anything and everything is now possible

As I embrace these Divine properties within I feel them permeate throughout every cell, atom, and molecule of my entire body and then I feel them move up through my chakras and ignite the light of divinity within my third eye.

As this light is ignited I feel a lightness of being and a connection to all that is.

I feel this light radiate outward from the center of my brow and then connect to all of life.

I feel oneness with all that is and I become one with it. As I do I see the world now through the eyes of love.

I release any preconceived notion of separateness that I might have been harboring and now accept that I AM one with all that is and all that will ever be.

I send this prayer up to the divine realm with an attitude of gratitude that Spirit has answered my every call.

Thank you Mother- Father God it is done"

This third eye is also known as the 'eye of Siva' which is the organ of spiritual vision located in the middle of your forehead. We evolve in our karma through our third eye in our evolution of spirit. As we continue to evolve in our evolution of spirit, further out of matter or the physical, and back into spirit and the divine light of creation, we will then achieve spiritual awareness that will transport us beyond time and space, at which point spiritual ascension will occur. In meditation and prayer the pineal gland is lifted out of its stagnant state back into the light. It is through our evolution of spirit that this gland also evolves into the awareness of the non-physical world and of our higher self and then activates the light within. This evolution of spirit is often represented by the thousand-fold lotus, which represents our awakening within and our inner vision. The third eye has throughout history been associated with mystical powers and has also been connected to the realm of thought; if you think it you can create it. When awakened this seat of consciousness awakens the light within and connects you to God.

It's also important to denote that this symbol of the all-seeing eye has always been part of the earth's creational mythologies and mysteries. It can be found on the back of our dollar bill where the third eye resides within the great pyramid of Giza. Isn't it interesting that the pineal gland, which represents the third eye, is located in the exact geometric center of the brain which correlates directly to the location of the great pyramid of Giza in the geophysical center of our planet; which is also known as the foundation stone for our world ?

Our Forefathers indeed knew and practiced these spiritual mysteries. When we focus on the Holy Trinity of these three glands we connect with God and the divine realm and the possibilities are then endless as to what we can accomplish.

Do not confuse your mind with your brain. Your brain is simply your computer while your mind sits about 18 inches above your head and connects you directly to the divine realm. When we go into meditation we need to turn off the static in the brain and move into the expansion of the mind where true connection to spirit occurs. We need to quiet all the chatter and static and listen with our heart. We listen with our hearts because the Angels communicate with us through our heart chakra. Our heart chakra is the seat of the soul. It is where the Holy Spirit entered our bodies at first breath and began the heart to beat. It is within this chakra that God resides within us all. God and the Holy Spirit are represented within this chakra by the color pink, which is love, the color gold which is wisdom and the color blue which is divine will. These three rays of light when combined become the violet consuming flame, which then connects us to the divine realm, to our own spirit guides, to the seven Elohim of creation and the omnipresent God.

When we are connected as such in meditation or prayer all questions become answered and whatever you can imagine will then become your reality. As we evolve in our spiritual ascension we become aware of just how connected we truly all are. We also become aware of how accessible the divine realm is. The divine Masters and Archangels are there for us. To gain their assistance all we have to do is ask. It is really that simple. When we ask for their help, help is then at our fingertips. When we honor ourselves and go within the temple of our bodies to connect in spirit to the divine realm, our lives are then changed and we begin our true evolution of spirit.

I implore you to go within and invoke the assistance of the divine realm through the prayers given to you within this chapter or through whatever method works for you. In your spiritual quest reach for the stars, leave no stone unturned, for the illumination of spirit when achieved becomes a window into the soul and is our most profound gift we can give ourselves.

CHAPTER 4

ST. GERMAIN & SPIRITUAL ALCHEMY

"Everyone thinks of changing the world, but no one thinks of changing himself."

- Leo Tolstoy -

At the beginning of the twentieth century a group of souls integrated onto the earth plane to pave the way for others to follow. This dedicated soul group began to examine and unravel the mysteries of the universe. They were the peaceful warriors who were the forerunners of the Indigo Children. The collective consciousness at that time was very closed and a churchianity prevailed that closed off even the possibility of a higher truth that was not intertwined with exact church doctrines. These souls worked diligently and quietly to bring divine truths to the surface so they could be seen and embraced. These truths were unraveling the illusions of separateness and beginning to embrace the reality of oneness. In the 1930's, Guy W. Ballard, while hiking in northern California, met the Ascended Master, Saint Germain on the side of Mt. Shasta. His remarkable experiences were recorded in the books "Unveiled Mysteries" and "The Magic Presence" written under the pen name of Godfre King. These were first published in 1934 and are known as the "I Am Discourses". These discourses have never been out of print. They were meant to be a tool to assist mankind in his spiritual evolution into the light of God's divine plan for the individual and for the collective whole of all nations as well as for future generations to come. They are a teaching tool to illuminate the way into divine love and into true alchemy of spirit. In the book "Saint Germain on Alchemy, Formulas for Self-Transformation" by Mark L. Prophet and Elizabeth Clare Prophet, there is a quote by Saint Germain. "The inner meaning of alchemy is simply all-composition, implying the relation of the all of the creation to the parts which compose it. Thus alchemy, when properly understood, deals with the conscious power of controlling mutations and transmutations within matter and energy and even within life itself. It is the science of the mystic and it is the forte of the self-realized man who, having sought, has found himself to be one with God and is willing to play his part".

To many Saint Germain is known as the patron saint of alchemy wherein it was said he could turn base metals into gold. Yet Saint Germain's greatest legacy lies in his ability to transform the baser and negative traits of mankind into the positive traits of spiritual enlightenment and ascension of spirit. It is from his ascended state that he bestows upon us all the ultimate gift of freedom, the violet consuming flame.

Known as the master alchemist, Saint Germain bestows upon all who pray to him or invoke his help through the spoken word, with the vehicles for self-transformation. Self-transformation comes about through spiritual alchemy whereby we change the lead and drossness of negative energy into the gold and light of divine energy by invoking the use of the violet flame. This violet flame is as stated earlier, the power and authority on this planet for the next ten thousand years and was reintroduced into our presence at the dawn of the Aquarian Age in the year 2000.

The Aquarian Age is no longer about karma but is now about an instant response to a negative. We are now being required to be responsible for every negative that man has created. We must now return back to our divinity and begin to negate all the negativity we have ever created upon our planet. After centuries of keeping the violet consuming flame hidden and only shown to a very small group of spiritual adepts, Saint Germain, the divine realm, the Archangels and the Great White Brotherhood of Ascended Masters are working with the light bearers to release its power and authority into the world during this critical time in our collective spiritual evolution.

In the 'Voice of the I Am' in January, 1941 on Page 20, Saint Germain said, "The understanding, the knowledge and the use of the violet consuming flame through prayer and invocation is more valuable to mankind than all the jewels, gold and collective wealth on this planet." The prayer's and meditation's given in Chapter 3 will help you bring the violet consuming flame into your presence.

In an article by the Summit Lighthouse entitled 'St. Germain's Gift, The Violet Flame' it is stated, "The violet flame works a little like soap. Soap gets dirt out of your clothes by using the positive and negative charges of atoms. It works because each of its molecules has two sides – a side that is attracted to dirt and a side that is attracted to water. The dirt loving side attracts the dirt, like a magnet attracts paperclips when it is dragged through a box of them. The water-loving side sticks to the water carrying the dirt with it.

When we invoke the violet flame it sets up a polarity between the nucleus of the atom and the white fire core of the flame. The nucleus, being matter, assumes the negative pole; the white fire core of the violet flame, being spirit, assumes the positive pole.

The interaction between the nucleus of the atom and the light in the violet flame establishes an oscillation. This oscillation dislodges the densities that are trapped between the electrons orbiting the nucleus. As this hardened substance that weighs down the atom is loosened, it is thrown into the violet flame and carried away. But unlike soap, the violet flame does not simply surround and remove the debris. It transforms it into pure light-energy. Freed of this debris, the electrons begin to move freely, thus raising our vibration and propelling us into a more spiritual state of being."

The violet flame transmutes all negative back into the light of the divine. It transcends all belief structures, all creeds, and all genetics. When we invoke the violet flame into our beings it moves into us and through us and as it does it dislodges and carries away with it all negative emotions and physical dis-eases of the body. The wonder of the violet flame is that it transmutes all negative energy back into positive energy therefore restoring us back to spiritual purity and moving us into a total spiritual ascension of being. This use of the violet flame is the covenant of universal law and when invoked performs miracles for all who understand and use it.

Saint Germain in his teachings through many masters has said that miracles are manifest through the precise application of divine laws. His mission is always one of the gifts of peace, enlightenment, spiritual transformation and individual and collective freedom for the world. It is also important to denote that Saint Germain is known as the patron Saint of the United States of America. His mission has always remained the same no matter what century the truths were revealed, grasped and understood. He has always said" the power to change resides within every man; that each man, woman and child must become aware of their choices and either choose freedom, peace and enlightenment or choose fetters and limitations that will ultimately mire them down into an abyss of darkness".

When we choose freedom and the light over ignorance and darkness we will feel the quickening of the flame of freedom within our souls and move into a higher state of consciousness. This higher state of consciousness enables us to see the bigger picture. It pulls us out of the box we have put ourselves in and opens up all doorways to perception. It opens all portals to spiritual enlightenment. The alchemy and ascension of spirit brings to each of us freedom, peace and enlightenment. When we entrap ourselves within the confinement of baser needs and temporary pleasures, we abdicate our spiritual consciousness and our connection to the divine realm and we lose our way. Within our core and within our heart centers each of us has all the wisdom, strength, courage and skill we need to transcend in consciousness and into spiritual enlightenment. It is imperative we monitor and control our thought patterns every second of every day as those thought patterns then become our collective reality. All negative thought patterns are being pushed to the surface to be eradicated, transformed and transmuted back into the light all over our planet. None are exempt.

There is a spiritual awakening that is transpiring at this point in our collective history. Within this movement millions of souls are genuinely striving through collective consciousness to bring about peace, abundance and joy for all. We need to wake up and realize the people who are so willing now to deprive us of our livelihoods and life styles are a very small majority and we all need to exercise our rights and stand up and rise as one united collective front and take back our power! As we collectively exercise our rights for change through whatever venues or avenues that are available to us, through the avenue of the peaceful warrior, our governments that do not conform to our united and collective wishes will become obsolete. They will be replaced with a new government embracing the wisdom of our Founding Fathers that states a perfect government should be of the people, by the people and for the people.

We need to understand all power is interrelated. All power is subject to the laws of relativity. The primary types of power are physical, mental, emotional and spiritual. We also have temporal power wherein social influences and massive pressures are thrown at us by our governments and the churchianities of our world. Yet, few among us are aware of our degree of total power that God bestowed upon us in the gift of consciousness. As Saint Germain states in Book Three, Chapter One, Page 271 of 'Saint Germain on Alchemy', "Few are aware that they possess the power of focalization and intensification in the proper exercise of their attention through individual consciousness; nor do they realize that the interpretive and discriminate action of the God self enables them to take firm hold of the reins of power, to be in control of their lives, and to be less distracted by the social and karmic responsibilities that are daily thrust upon them."

In simple terms all four of your bodies are receptacles of the power of the violet consuming flame; you're physical, emotional, mental and etheric bodies absorb and then emanate this power. It is through the balancing of these four bodies in conjunction with your seven energy centers that this power of spirit can then flow through you and become one with you. This inner power that all of us possess is governed by our embracement of deeper truths and the recognition of sinister forces that are afoot in our world. As we recognize these sinister forces it behooves us to realize we are totally responsible and in charge of our thoughts and our decisions on the correct interpretation and usage of this power. While we cannot erase past lifetimes, the violet consuming flame has the power to erase or transmute the cause, the effect, the record and the memory of all our past mistakes. It is the only power that can eliminate all human negativity. It can blaze consume and purify all human negativity you have ever created in any time frame, in any dimension and in any universe, both known and unknown that you have ever created within your physical, mental, emotional and etheric bodies. That is how powerful the violet consuming flame is when invoked. It has the power to lift your soul up in consciousness of love, light, peace, joy, freedom and purification. This violet consuming flame changes negative energy into positive energy. It transforms darkness into light and fate into opportunity. As stated earlier it works by changing vibrations and is the single most powerful tool of self-transformation. Spiritual alchemy is the process by which we raise our spiritual vibrations into a total unity within the divine realm, and the love and light of creation. When we do this, we become one with the divine realm. Not only does the violet flame cleanse away all the negativity we have ever created, it also helps us become peaceful warriors. When we become advocates of change through our evolution of spirit there is nothing we cannot accomplish. When we couple this with compassion, understanding, patience and unconditional love we quite simply can change the world.

Deborah Fields

CHAPTER 5

THE INDIGO CHILDREN AND THE TRUTH OF THE PLANET

"The destination is not as important as the journey."

-Unknown-

When the Indigo Children began to integrate into the earth plane, a great awakening began to occur. These highly advanced souls, through free choice, began the journey that all of us are now embarking upon. They held the torch to light the way for everyone to follow.

These advanced souls are referred to as Indigo Children due to the purple and indigo that radiates from their auras. A group of these souls arrived at the turn of the century to prepare the path for the ones to come later. These souls are of the highest vibration in humanity and it is due to this vibration that the universe and the divine realm both demand and expect a great deal from them. They are the lightbearers and the truthbearers. They are the architects and teachers of our planet and are even now working together to shed the light into the darkness and to reflect back the truth of divinity, unity and unconditional love for all. They are collectively working together to bring illumination into the abyss of ignorance; to bring hope into a world immersed in despair. All are working diligently and coming together now in a unity of spirit to help facilitate the change that is sweeping the planet.

These Indigo Children will come from every sector of life, from every corner of the planet, from every nationality and economic background. They will be from the mighty and powerful as well as from the lowly and humble. They are jointly working together to wake up the planet. Our planet needs this wake-up call. It is well past the time where we can do business as usual. Change is in the air.

These Indigos are the ones who are being held accountable by the universal mind of God. They are being forced to stand up for what is right and to make changes upon this planet we all call home. They are shouting out to everyone who will listen that the mess we currently are in will no longer be tolerated.

These are the movers and shakers of the world. They are demanding change on a grand scale as well as a much smaller scale. You may instinctively recognize them and be drawn to their energy. People will come to them for comfort, knowledge, advice, and for answers.

These truly advanced souls were born with many blessings. Some are healers and are collectively healing the heart and soul of humanity through their meditations and visualizations of a more loving and positive world. They heal the body, mind and spirit. Some are clairvoyant and see a higher vibratory dimension. They see the truth of the world; they see things as they are and not as we sometimes perceive them to be. Some are clairsentient and sense the cries of the universe, our planet and humanity. They are working together to soothe, heal and protect. Some are clairaudient and hear a higher frequency, a higher voice, a higher truth. They hear the call of the universe that is demanding that "now" is the time to awaken humanity. Some are gifted and blessed with all four gifts and theirs is the heaviest of all burdens for they are the ones who are leading the way and they carry upon their shoulders the hope of the world.

These souls will accomplish the awakening of humanity through many different avenues. They will reach you through the movies you watch that provoke you to embrace a new idea, a new thought that will then alter your state of consciousness. They will reach you through the books you read, the television shows you see and through the teachers you admire and follow. You will connect with them in ways you won't even understand but when you hear their message it will resonate within your being as the truth. When this happens there will be a quickening that is born within the center of your being, an excitement that tells you that you're where you need to be and are hearing your inner truth and are on your pathway to enlightenment.

These souls bear the light for humanity and will galvanize mankind into taking up the challenges of environmental awareness, of political and corporate corruption, of the discovery of new energy sources that burn clean energy and of judicial corruption. They are working hard in all sectors to turn on the light to the truth of the planet.

The truth of the planet is that our beautiful world is a living and breathing entity. She is feminine energy. She is our mother earth our nurturer and provider. She is a truly holy entity and is connected to all that is and is a perfect reflection of the glory and beauty of God. Without her support and protection we would all cease to exist. She is the foundation that our world is built upon.

Ed McGaa who is known as Eagleman and is an Oglala Sioux lawyer, writer and lecturer wrote this amazing piece of work entitled, "In Mother Earth Spirituality, Native American Paths to Healing Ourselves and Our Worlds". In this work he states, "Our survival is dependent on the realization that Mother Earth is a truly holy being, that all the things in this world are holy and must not be violated and that we must share and be generous with one another. You may call this thought by whatever fancy words you wish – psychology, theology, sociology or philosophy – but you must think of Mother Earth as a living being. Think of your fellow men and women as holy people who were put here by the Great Spirit. Think of being related to all things! With this philosophy in mind as we go on with our environmental ecology efforts, our search for spirituality, and our quest for peace, we will be far more successful when we truly understand the Indian's respect for Mother Earth." When we collectively unite as one and begin to honor and respect Mother Earth, then she in turn will honor and respect us. When we honor and respect the earth she showers us with abundance. When we defile, desecrate, contaminate and pollute her, she weeps for our lack of reverence and holds back her bounty. When our actions elicit a reaction from Mother Earth due to our arrogance and carelessness, she will rear up and cleanse what we have tried to destroy. In this cleansing process she will renew herself and get rid of the pollution that we have created. In the process our crops are destroyed due to floods and whole food supplies are contaminated, compromised and famine occurs. Our homes and businesses are destroyed by fires, mudslides, tornados and hurricanes and whole populations are displaced and livelihoods are lost. Does any of this sound familiar to you? We need to pay attention and wake up! Mother Earth will only tolerate so much abuse. If we don't begin to honor her, more disasters will occur and this is global! It is not just happening to some of us, it is happening to all of us!

Look at Katrina, at the earthquakes that rocked China and Japan, at the tsunami that struck with devastating results in the Indian Ocean, at the mudslides in California, the fires all over the world and the tornados that decimated the Midwest and southern states of The United States. Unless we wake up and begin to honor Mother Earth, more of these will occur.

Through our collective thoughts and actions we have contributed to these disasters that have been occurring with alarming frequency. Here is a universal truth, "Our thought patterns directly control our environment and our weather patterns". Think of the power of that statement and be responsible for monitoring your thoughts. What you think emotes from you and creates your environment and either uplifts or pollutes your world. Our thoughts have life. They circle around us much as the moon orbits the earth. When they are left unresolved they can wreak havoc and create great damage. We need to begin to monitor more closely the thoughts we have and change our negative thoughts into positive ones. We need to resolve these negative thoughts with a shift of attitude as they create a heavy and toxic burden that we carry around with us. It is this burden that is responsible for all dis-eases of the mind and emotions that then pollutes and corrupts the body. When we release these toxic emotions they dissipate and return once again to the light and we are enlightened. We are literally then lighter in being.

Those who refuse to honor Mother Earth, who refuse to see the truth of the planet, will be removed. Everyone will be given the choice to believe or to not believe; to embrace or not to embrace. The choice will be to move forward into the change that is occurring or to remain behind. This choice given will directly determine a soul's future existence upon this planet. So choose wisely.

Yet, even through this dire warning, all is not lost. This is not an end, but a beginning. Everyone will be given the tools they need to move forward on the road to enlightenment. Pay attention because what is given and what is offered will be exactly what is needed to move us all forward into this new earth and new way of being.

It all begins with each and every one of us when we accept the possibility of the truth in what is being given, in the truth in what is heard and in what is written. It all begins when we acknowledge that our environment is in trouble and we begin to honor, respect and revere Mother Earth before we too become as extinct as the dinosaurs.

We need to ask ourselves some serious questions. What is my role in this environmental disaster that is currently plaguing our planet? What can I do in my life to help change this course of events? Where do I begin and what does that look like to me? How do I begin the process of healing my world?

We begin to heal the world and stem the bleeding by first and foremost acknowledging our part in the process, by becoming accountable for our thoughts and actions, and by forgiving whatever our transgressions are that led us to where we are today.

You may ask yourselves these questions; do I help protect the environment by using more eco-friendly light bulbs to conserve energy until new and improved energy sources are introduced on the planet? Do I protect the air we breathe by lobbying against coal plants that do not convert bad air to clean air? Do I begin by changing my automobile to an eco-friendly vehicle that protects the environment? Do I begin by planting two trees for every tree that is cut down so the oxygen supply on this amazing exquisite planet is not compromised? Do I begin by not polluting the waters of the earth so our water supply is not contaminated? Do I begin to honor and respect Mother Earth so she in turn will honor and respect me? Only you know the answers to these questions. I implore you to go within and find your truth. These will be our challenges. These will be our choices and they are some of the most important choices we will ever make. It is time to move forward and cleanse our world. It is time to monitor our thoughts moment by moment, second by second and cleanse our bodies. It is time to embrace the change that is occurring and become that change in motion because when we do, we are all cleansed. When we do, we are all saved.

CHAPTER 6

OUR ASCENSION

OF SPIRIT

"Don't lose hope. When it gets darkest the stars come out."

-Unknown-

In the realm of the divine there is absolute rejoicing when even one of us finds and begins to walk our true path of enlightenment. Our journey to enlightenment is the most important journey we will ever embark upon. Our ascension of spirit along the pathway of this incredible journey is the direct road marker in the evolution of our soul. When we ascend in spirit we define and redefine our spiritual blueprint, which is always in flux. At the end of this amazing journey we will have fulfilled our contract and our mission upon the earth plane. The choices we make along the way are what define us. The choices we make along the way either lead us to the light of divinity or into the abyss of negativity. We are all so much more than we seem. We are all so much more powerful than we could ever imagine. The biggest question along this journey will be who am I? And who do I want to become? The most important quest along the road in this journey will be to hear the voice of God within us.

Sri Chinmoy eloquently said, "For those who follow the spiritual life there comes a time when we distinctly hear God's voice. God offers us his highest message; today's imperfect man is tomorrow's perfect God. Today's unfulfilled man becomes tomorrow's fulfilled God. But how? Through divine love, divine devotion and divine surrender."

This ascension of spirit is the process through which the soul and the human being's personality become totally integrated as one and transcend back into the divine love and light of creation.

This ascension and enlightenment of spirit is the only job any of us ever has. It is a job a lot of humanity has abdicated in favor of the baser needs of the body. While these needs are certainly important to our overall wellbeing, the abdication of spirit is a disaster to our evolution. It is important to find a synergy between the two and to merge and integrate all four bodies and all seven energy centers into one of perfect balance and harmony. When we have this synergy between our four bodies and our seven chakras they collectively provide the vehicle through which our soul journeys through time and space. When we honor and respect this process we honor and respect our soul's journey into spiritual evolution and in the process we bring harmony and balance into our lives.

Sri Chinmoy has said, "Spirituality is not an escape from the world of reality. Spirituality tells us what the true reality is and how we can discover it here on earth. Spirituality is not the denial of life, but the purest acceptance of life. Life is to be accepted unreservedly. Life is to be realized soulfully. Life is to be transformed totally. Life is to be lived eternally".

It is imperative that we stop polluting our bodies with negativity. We all need to release the negative and embrace the positive. When we hold on to negative emotions we totally pollute the body with energy that emotes from the dark side. These negative energies are responsible for all dis-ease of the body. These negative energies create a total disconnect of spirit and create unending static and interference within the mind. Trying to get through all of that negativity is similar to opening three years of e-mails and the divine Masters and the Angelic realm simply cannot go there! When we embrace negativity and turn away from the light, the divine realm cannot communicate with us. The Angels have said if there is a deceiver upon this planet it resides between the ears! When we pollute our systems with fear, doubt, depression, apathy and anger we create static and confusion in our brains that creates a virus very similar to the viruses that afflict our computers.

This pollution of the senses has become an epidemic in our world in the degeneration of spirit amongst those who feel lost and abandoned. For those lost in despair, feeling trapped in a world they themselves have created there is hope. Holding on to fear, anger, resentment or any emotion derived from fear simply robs you of your energy, of your life force. It creates heaviness in your heart and manifests itself in illness and in a dis-ease of your body. It causes you depression and moves you into a downward spiral of despair, which then blocks the incredible beauty of the world around you.

It is far more productive for us to take a good look at our anger and resentment and find its inner truth. For truth always lies within us. Do not berate yourself for harboring a negative feeling. Rather examine it, acknowledge it, embrace it and release it. Remember we always have a choice. At all times we can either choose love or fear and always remember resentment is just another form of fear.

There is a universal truth that is so simple and yet so perfect in it's absolute simplicity. "There are no dark or evil forces at work, there is only ignorance." Ignorance breeds fear and fear then creates what we perceive as darkness and evil. All things; everything we see, think and imagine are of God, from God and are of the light. God is the light. We are all beings of the light. We are all beings of God. When we evolve in spirit and walk in the light we then become accustomed to the brilliance and can see the face of God. When we see the face of God in its entire splendor we see God in everything and we experience true peace of being. We experience and create true peace in our worlds and in our realities.

When we release this anger and resentment we move out of the darkness of ignorance and into the brilliance of hope. For those who feel lost in depression and despair there is hope. All of us need to help bridge a path from despair to hope. We need to build a bridge of hope supported by unconditional love and washed in the light of divinity so that those who seem to be lost can find their way home. We need to reach out and shine a beacon of brilliant light into the abyss of darkness and ignorance. We need to shine the light of hope into the darkness. With this beacon of hope comes possibility and opportunity.

Whenever you see someone who is depressed and in despair never turn your back! Always reach out and help even if that form of help is only a kind word of encouragement. That one kind word may give that soul just the boost it needs in order to move back into the light of hope. For after all, hope is all that is needed to move the soul back into the light of understanding, compassion and unconditional love. Hope is the life line that when cast out saves the soul from the vortex of despair.

When just one of us offers words of encouragement, compassion and understanding we uplift the spirit of the one who seems lost and we are all uplifted. We need to reach out to those who are in despair and offer a better reality. We need to shine the light of possibility into the darkest recesses of their minds so the seeds of negativity and ignorance are totally eradicated. When we do this we have a cleansing of spirit. It is our challenge to bring hope and enlightenment to those in need and to open up the doorway to change wherein the reality for all shifts and hope begins to sparkle and shine for all to see. When we throw out a lifeline to those in need we are all saved.

We then begin to alter the reality of the afflicted from the illusion of what was to the reality of what is. Then all negativity is washed away in the rain of hope and unconditional love.

Be aware of your own contribution of emotion that either uplifts or pollutes the whole. Be cognizant that all of us have at some point in our spiritual journey floundered and lost our way. We have all needed a helping hand and a kind word to set us back upon our path. Think about what your life would have been like if someone had not thrown you a lifeline!

Look into the mirror of life and embrace the image reflected back. If you don't like what you see simply change it. Change the way you perceive the world. Replace negative thoughts with positive ones. All it takes is just one of us to begin the process. All it takes is one kind word to another to begin the chain of hope. All it takes is one helping hand to continue the circle of life and to begin the quickening of the spirit into the brilliance of enlightenment.

Your power is infinite. Embrace it as it can never be disconnected. It is everlasting. Your power to create is your sacred treasure dwelling deep within the recesses of your soul. This power is your 'I Am'. This 'I Am' is your spark of divinity animating the body and illuminating the soul. It resides within your heart which is your true creator of all abundance. It is the seat of unconditional love and is the seat of the soul. It is your compassion, your infinite wisdom, your power within. We are now present here in this infinite moment of time and space in order to know the unconditional love contained within the 'I Am' presence residing within all of us. It is this 'I Am' presence that dances to the melody of the ethers and sings the song of unity; I am one, I am all powerful, I am all loving, I am all perfection, I am all light, I am....

Deborah Fields

CHAPTER 7

HARMONIC RESONANCE

"Don't be afraid of the space between your dreams and reality. If you can dream it, you can make it so."

-Belva Davis-

Each and every one of us has within our being the divine light of creation that dances and sings the forgotten melodies within every cell, atom and molecule in our bodies. This is our link to our individual divinity and is our direct access to the portal of the divine realm.

This divine light of creation within each of us is our spiritual matrix, which defines the blueprint of our souls. This blueprint is the road map to our divinity and defines who we are and how we have evolved. It is this road map that gives each of us our own unique stamp of individuality.

All of life gathers its spark of animation from this Divine light of creation. It is what makes us all multi-dimensional. All life forms within the universe both known and unknown vibrate within this Divine light. It is this living light that is then translated to the energy of all matter. This living light that is found in all matter resonates within all life forms .This is called harmonic resonance. Nothing in our Universe would exist without it. It is this harmonic resonance that then vibrates to the beautiful melody of the ethers.

Within the field of quantum physics it is widely recognized that all living life-forms and all material objects vibrate to a unique individual frequency of what is defined as angstrom units per second. It is this living energy force that is directly responsible for the universal harmony and synchronicity of life. When we raise our individual angstrom units per second we are essentially raising our vibrations and in the process are evolving in spirit. It is this process of raising our vibrations through prayer, meditation, invocation, supplication and also through a communion with nature and the universal mind of God that propels us forward in our spiritual journey towards enlightenment. Anyone of the prayers or mantras that were given in the beginning of this book can help you achieve this enlightenment of spirit.

The revered scientist Nicola Tesla who lived over one hundred and fifty years ago understood and knew how to harness the vibrations of the universe. Tesla stated, "All matter comes from a primary substance, the luminous ethers." He saw the universe as an amazing cosmos composed and held in place by a symphony of alternating currents. He deeply felt he would be closer to a more comprehensive understanding of the universe if he understood the electrical vibrations and their complete range of function within the infinite cosmos. He saw a cosmic symphony played out in harmonic resonance that existed in all objects whether they were inanimate or animate. Tesla concluded absolutely nothing would exist within the universe without harmonic resonance and he was absolutely correct. During his lifetime a churchianity and closed-mindedness existed that labeled him as eccentric due to his seemingly unbelievable and bizarre claims within the scientific community. For this he was ostracized and looked upon as a mad scientist. In actuality he is regarded by many to be the father of physics and the man who invented the twentieth century. Nicola Tesla was responsible for the discovery and development of AC or alternating current that we all use in our homes today. In 1893

Tesla demonstrated on a low scale the effect of wireless energy transfer to wirelessly powered electronic devices through the use of light bulbs. He worked with and totally understood electromagnetism and electromechanical engineering. Tesla has in varying degrees contributed to the establishment of robotics, remote control, radar, computer science and to the expansion of ballistics, nuclear physics and theoretical physics. In 1943, after his death, the supreme court of the United States credited him as being the inventor of the radio rather than Guglielmo Marconi.

During Tesla's lifetime he devised methods of wireless transmissions of energy that worked compatibly with both electromagnetic fields as well as with harmonic resonance. This amazing man worked intimately within areas of science and physics that moved beyond our imagination and concept of time and space. He believed in the magic of the universe and that the universe vibrated and resonated with light and sound.

It is said by many that Tesla's hearing was so acute he could hear a fly land on a table as an explosion of sound within his inner ear that was excruciatingly painful for him. Due to this extreme sensitivity to sound he could accurately hear the melody of the ethers and this along with his amazing ability to visualize and picture the entire blueprint to an idea in one flash right down to it's most minute of details, made Tesla one of the greatest scientists of our world. His contributions were many but it was his work with and his complete understanding of matter and harmonic resonance that truly linked this great man with the divine realm and universal law. His understanding that all matter was born directly from the divine realm shows his complete comprehension of the universe. He saw the universe as a vast frequency of love and light played out within a spiritual matrix that when tapped into could produce amazing works of genius. He was able to tap into the universal mind and grasp complicated concepts and great truths much like Albert Einstein and has left an indelible mark upon mankind.

He sensed the vibrations of the universe and understood that these vibrations played out upon the stage of the cosmos in a symphony of light and sound that was constantly in flux and in perpetual motion, every second realigning itself into more beautiful and complex patterns. He totally understood that the universe was constantly shifting and redefining itself in a dance of creation.

We are currently experiencing a massive vibratory shift upon this planet. This shift is wreaking havoc and is in the process sweeping away all negative systems and belief structures no longer functioning. Although this process is very painful for us all, at the end of the day a renewed and healed world order will emerge and with it a new harmonic vibration will resonate on our planet bringing order and balance to the universe.

We have been spinning out of control in a negative vibration that has been collectively created. We are now being aided and assisted not only from the divine realm but also from the universe itself. Many believe there are beings that exist within the scope of the universe who are here and present at this historical shift upon our planet. These beings of light exist within galaxies in the universe that move beyond our comprehension. These beings of love and light are often referred to as star people, aliens or simply ETs.

Within our collective histories we have legends that have been passed down from generation to generation of the existence of beings outside our planet. There are also many startling documentations of human beings claiming to have seen, encountered and been abducted by these star people or ETs. Recorded history and archeological findings show us ancient civilizations that believed in the existence of star people. Within the Old Testament in the book of Ezekiel there is such a recording. Within this book the prophet Ezekiel gives an account of seeing a flaming chariot that descended in the desert and landed beside the river Chebar in Babylon. Sound like a UFO to you? He states within these pages that this chariot was the color of metal and was surrounded by fire that enfolded itself. He describes how there were four objects that came out of this mysterious cloud that had a wheel within a wheel with a ring of eyes. Four man-like creatures in suits of burnished brass with crystal firmaments on their heads emerged from this chariot.

All of this was recorded in the sixth century! I'll leave it up to you to decide what you feel Ezekiel saw and recorded. However, to me it sounds very much like he was possibly describing a flying saucer and an encounter with alien beings.

In Indian Sanskrit there are texts providing evidence in the classic Vedic and Hindu writings of metallic flying machines called 'vimanas'. There have been many discoveries throughout the ages of the unexplainable. From the cave drawings and primitive carvings found throughout the world of beings dressed in startling contemporary fashions, as has been discovered in Lussac, France, to crop circles discovered world-wide especially in southern England, to the volcanic monolithic heads on Easter Island, to the megalithic monument of Stonehenge, there is an abundance of startling evidence of beings who not only existed but left behind their mark on our civilization. Who were these beings? Where did they come from? What were they trying to accomplish and what was their message? These are questions for the ages.

In my channeling I'm told by my guides that mankind has throughout the ages been visited by an Extraterrestrial Brotherhood of Light known by many as star people or ETs and will continue to be visited throughout all of time and beyond. They have told me that it is absolutely ludicrous for us to believe we are the only life form within this universe and that our planet exists within the 12th universe within God's infinite Cosmos. Our universe is the largest of the all the other universes that have preceded it, and has the greatest variety of learning and growth opportunities for humanity. Most of the life forms within our universe exist within a 5th dimensional reality therefore cannot be detected with a 3rd dimensional eye. We need to evolve in spirit before we will be able to see the marvels and wonders that co-exist within Gods world. They have told me the Arcturians who are beings of love and light have been visiting and helping humanity for ages in the evolution of the human spirit. The Arcturians are one of the most advanced groups of extraterrestrials in the galaxy. They originated from the star Arcturus, which is the brightest star in the Bootes constellation. They are known and believed by many to be the almighty healers of the universe and are known as the spiritual leaders of humanity.

Edgar Casey, the renowned psychic of the 40's, stated that "Arcturus is the most advanced civilization in our entire galaxy". Casey also said, "The Arcturians are a fifth dimensional life form that is highly advanced both technically and spiritually". There is a belief they have totally transcended the spiritual plane and reside at the throne of God. It is also believed they are an energy gateway through which humanity must pass through during the death and rebirth transcension. They function as a way station if you will, for the non-physical consciousness to become accustomed to the physical restraints of the human body. They are highly spiritual beings who are present here now to aid, assist and move us along our pathway to spiritual evolution and the ascension process. They are now playing a key role in the shift of vibratory harmonics enveloping our planet. They are of the light and from the divine mind of God and anyone can call upon them to aid and assist in the healing process of each of us individually and in the healing process of the collective whole of humanity. There is a book written about the Arcturian healing technologies from the higher dimensions called "The 250 Golden Keys to Creating Perfect Radiant Health in Your Physical Body from the Soul's Perspective" by Dr. Joshua David Stone. I highly recommend it to anyone who is interested in calling upon the Arcturians and Lord Arcturus who is the first of the mighty Elohim to come to your aid and to help heal your mind, body and spirit.

You can choose to believe in the existence of these amazing beings or choose not to. I leave that totally up to you. But, who knows, one thing we can all attest to is a multiplicity of unexplainable phenomena that has left a lot of us baffled and scratching our heads.

I'm told these beings of light are here to help us once again as our planet moves into the vibratory harmonics of the Aquarian Age. These beings are working in conjunction with the divine realm to help humanity evolve. It is through their collective efforts we will all experience a spiritual rebirth that will propel us into a state of divine awareness. It is within this state of divine awareness we will collectively eradicate the deep pockets of negativity currently existing upon our planet. It is through this process we will lift up the collective consciousness to one of divine hope, unconditional love and to a total awareness of the sacredness of all life. When this occurs we will hold up the mirror of our own divinity so all can be enlightened and each spark of the divine residing within us can be reflected back.

In my own quest for truth I was given by an enlightened being, an email written by Patricia Cota-Robels on March 18, 2008. There is a saying when the student is ready the teacher will come. Well, I can totally attest to this profound truth and have on many occasions experienced just that. In this email entitled "A Critical Time for the USA and Mother Earth" she states "From every being of light in the realms of truth, humanity is being guided to focus the power of our attention on the vision of the new earth in all her resplendent glory. In spite of the saber rattling and war drums we are being bombarded with by the media, every credible lightworker is gently turning his or her attention to the mission of co-creating heaven on Mother Earth…..HOME. This is our purpose and reason for being and it is why we volunteered to be on Earth during this cosmic moment. We have been training for eons of time for this mission. Within our hearts we have all of the wisdom, strength, skill, courage and trust we need to succeed God victoriously. We must monitor our thoughts, words, feelings and actions daily and hourly to be sure we are empowering only the patterns of Heaven on Earth instead of the fragmented, fear-based thought forms that are being pushed to the surface all over the planet; to be healed and transmuted back into light. Every world religion has taught us in one way or another that we are responsible for the circumstances occurring in our lives. What we send out through our thoughts, words, actions and feelings returns to us. This is true whether we are focusing our attention on hate or love, poverty or abundance, disease or health, war or peace."

Within this same e-mail was a speech given by Congressman Dennis Kucinich, a democratic representative from Ohio, on June 9, 2002. This speech was given at the Praxis Peace Institute Conference in Dubrovnik, Croatia.

The message contained within this profound speech was so uplifting and amazing that I was urged by my guides to include it in its entirety. The following message was made even more profound because it was given by a member of Congress in a government that has forgotten it was elected by the people, for the people and of the people. So I end this chapter with this amazing speech entitled "Spirit and Stardust" by U.S. Representative Dennis Kucinich.

"As one studies the images of the Eagle Nebula brought back by the Hubble telescope from that place in deep space where stars are born, one can imagine the interplay of cosmic forces across space and time of matter and spirit dancing to the music of the spheres atop an infinite sea of numbers.

Spirit merges with matter to sanctify the universe. Matter transcends to return to spirit. The interchangeability of matter and spirit means the starlit magic of the outmost life of our universe becomes the soul-light magic of the innermost life of our self. The energy of the stars becomes us. We become the energy of the stars. Stardust and spirit unite and we begin: one with the universe - whole and holy from one source, endless creative energy bursting forth, kinetic, elemental – we, the earth, air, water and fire, source of nearly fifteen billion years of cosmic spiraling. We begin as a perfect union of matter and spirit. We receive the blessings of the Eternal from sky and earth. In our outstretched hands, we can feel the energy of the universe. We receive the blessings of the Eternal from water which nourishes and sanctifies life. We receive the blessings of the Eternal from the primal fire, the pulsating heart of creation. We experience the wonder of life, multi-dimensional and transcendent. We extend our hands upwards and we are showered with abundance. We ask and we receive. A universe of plenty flows to us, through us. It is in us. We become filled with endless possibilities.

We need to remember where we come from, to know that we are one, to understand that we are of an undivided whole: race, color, nationality, creed, gender are beams of light refracted through one great prism. We begin as perfect and journey through life to become more perfect in the singularity of "I" and in the multiplicity of "we", a more perfect union of matter and spirit. This is human striving. This is where, in Shelly's words…."hope creates from its own wreck the thing it contemplates". This is what Browning spoke of, our "reach exceeding our grasp". This is a search for Heaven within, a quest for our eternal home. In our souls magnificence we become conscious of the cosmos within us. We hear the music of peace; we hear the music of cooperation; we hear the music of love. We hear harmony; a celestial symphony in our souls. Forgetting, we become unconscious of our cosmic birthright. Plighted with disharmony, disunity, torn asunder from the stars in a disaster well described by Matthew Arnold in 'Dover Beach', "...the world, which seems to be before us like a land of dreams, so various, so beautiful, so new, hath really neither joy, nor love, nor light, nor certitude, nor peace, nor help for pain. And we are here, as on a darkling plane, swept with confused alarms of struggle and flight where ignorant armies clash by night." Today Dover Beach is up on the shores of the Potomac River in Washington, D.C. Our leaders think the unthinkable and speak of the unspeakable inevitably of nuclear war, of a nuclear attack on New York City, of terrorist attacks throughout our nation, of war against Iraq using nuclear weapons, of biological and chemical weapon attacks on civilian populations, of catastrophic global climate change, of war in outer space.

When death, not life, becomes inevitable, we are presented with an opportunity for great clarity for a great awakening, to rescue the human spirit from the arms of Morpheus through love, through compassion and through integrating spiritual vision and active citizenship to restore peace to our world. The moment that one world is about to end, a New World is about to begin. We need to remember where we come from because the path home is also the way to the future.

In Ohio, the state I represent in the United States Congress, there is a memorial to peace, named by its sculptor, Marshal A. Fredericks, the "Fountain of Eternal Life". A figure rises from the flames, his gaze fixed to the stars, his hands positioned sextant-like as if measuring the distance. Through fames of war from the millions of hearts and the dozens of places wherein it rages may lick at our consciousness, our gaze must be fixed upward to invoke universal principals of unity, cooperation, of compassion, to infuse our world with peace, to ask the active presence of peace, to expand our capacity to receive it and to express it in our everyday life. We must do this fearlessly and courageously and not breathe in the poison gas of terror. As we receive, so shall we give.

As citizen diplomats of the world, we send peace as conscious expression wherever, whenever and to whomever it is needed: to the Middle East, to the Israelis and the Palestinians, to the Pakistanis and the Indians, to Americans and to al-Quaida and to the people of Iraq and to all those locked in deadly combat. And we fly to be with the bereft, with those on the brink, to listen compassionately setting aside judgment and malice to become peacemakers, to intervene, to mediate, to bring ourselves back from the abyss, to bind up the world's wounds.

As we aspire to universal brotherhood and sisterhood, we hearken to the cry from the heart of the world and respond affirmatively to address through thought, word and deed conditions which give rise to conflict: economic exploitation, empire building, political oppression, religious intolerance, poverty, famine, homelessness, struggles over control of water, land, minerals and oil. We realize that what affects anyone anywhere affects everyone everywhere. As we help others to heal, we heal ourselves. Our vision of interconnectedness resonates with new networks of world citizens in non-governmental organizations linking from numberless centers of energy, expressing the emergence of a new organic whole, seeking unity within and across national lines. New transnational, web-based e-mail and telecommunications systems transcend governments and carry within them the power of qualitative transformation of social and political structures and a new sense of creative intelligence. If governments and their leaders bound by hierarchy and patriarchy, wedded to military might for legitimacy, fail to grasp the implications of an emerging world consciousness for cooperation, for peace and for sustainability, they may become irrelevant.

As citizen activists merge the world over, they can become an irresistible force to create peace and protect the planet. From here will come a new movement to abolish nuclear weapons and all weapons of mass destruction. From here will come the demand for sustainable communities, for new systems of energy, transportation and commerce. From here comes the future rushing in on us.

How does one acquire the capacity for active citizenship? The opportunities exist every day. In Cleveland, citizens have developed the ability to intercede when schools are scheduled to be closed and have kept the schools open. Citizens can rally to keep hospitals open, to save industries which provide jobs, to protect neighborhood libraries from curtailment of service, to improve community policing, to meet racial, ethnic and religious intolerance openly and directly.

Active citizenship begins with an envisioning of the desired outcome and a conscious application of spiritual principles. I know. I have worked with the people of my own community. I have seen the dynamic of faith in self, faith in one's ability to change things, faith in one's ability to prevail against the odds through an appeal to the spirit of the world for help, through an appeal to the spirit of community for participation, through an appeal to the spirit of cooperation which multiplies energy. I have seen citizens challenge without condemning anyone while invoking principles of non-opposition and inclusion of those who disagree.

I have seen groups of people overcome incredible odds as they become aware they are participating in a cause beyond self and sense the movement of the inexorable which comes from unity. When you feel this principal at work, when you see spiritual principles form the basis of active citizenship, you are reminded once again of the merging of stardust and spirit. There is creativity. There is magic. There is alchemy

Citizens across the United States are now uniting in a great cause to establish a Department of Peace, seeking nothing less than the transformation of our society, to make non-violence an organizing principle, to make war archaic through creating a paradigm shift in our culture for human development, for economic and political justice and for violence control. It's work in violence control will be to support disarmament treaties, peaceful co-existence and peaceful consensus building. It's focus on economic and political justice will examine and enhance resource distribution, human and economic rights and strengthen democratic values.

Domestically, the Department of Peace would address violence in the home, spousal abuse, child abuse, gangs, police/community relations, conflicts and work with individuals and groups to achieve changes in attitudes that examine the mythologies of cherished world views such as "violence is inevitable" or "war is inevitable". Thus it will help with the discovery of new selves and new paths toward peaceful consensus.

The Department of Peace will also address human development and the unique concerns of women and children. It will envision and seek to implement plans for peace education, not simply as a course of study but as a template for all pursuits of knowledge within formal educational settings.

Violence is NOT inevitable. War is NOT inevitable. Nonviolence and peace ARE inevitable. We can make this world a gift of peace, which will confirm the presence of universal spirit in our lives. We can send into the future the gift, which will protect our children from fear, from harm, from destruction. Carved inside the pediment, which sits atop the marble columns, is a sentinel at the entrance to the United States House of Representatives. Standing resolutely inside this "Apotheosis of Democracy" is a woman, a shield by her left side, with her outstretched right arm protecting a child happily sitting at her feet. This child holds the lamp of knowledge under the protection of this patroness.

This wondrous sculpture by Paul Wayland Bartlett is titled "Peace Protecting Genius". Not with nuclear arms, but with a loving maternal arm is the knowing child genius shielded from harm. This is the promise of hope over fear. This is the promise of love, which overcomes all. This is the promise of faith, which overcomes doubt. This is the promise of light, which overcomes darkness. This is the promise of peace, which overcomes war."

After reading this amazing speech I was left with a sense of awe and gratitude that there were individuals within the halls of government who could express so eloquently such a universal vision of hope, peace and unconditional love. In reading this profound speech one has sense of the divine light of creation dancing within the written word.

We all need to remember we began as a perfect union of matter and spirit vibrating in perfect harmony. We all need to reach out for the abundant blessings of the universe and create an environment of peace, love and hope for all. We need to realize the divine light of creation resides within each of our souls and the matrix of our realities is infused with harmonic resonance. It is this harmonic resonance that vibrates within our beings and gives animation to all of life. It is not just in some of us, but is in all of us. When we embrace this light within us, we become filled with infinite possibilities and here in this most sacred of places there is then magic. Here within the matrix of our being there is creativity, there is alchemy. Here in the center of our being we connect with all of life and we become whole. Here spirit and stardust merge to become one brilliant beam refracting all of life for us to see in one awe-inspiriting explosion of pure unconditional love.

Deborah Fields

CHAPTER 8

A RENEWAL OF LIGHT

"The moment you have in your heart this extraordinary thing called love and feel the depth, the delight, the ecstasy of it, you will discover that for you the world is transformed."

\- I. Krishnamurti -

Within the parameters of our world, what holds and binds us together are the divine properties of love and light. Now, at this moment in our collective history we have come to the point where all of the efforts that have been put forth within our spiritual evolution through time and space have now created a renewed level of light. Through this collective process there is now more light and a deeper awareness of this light. Through this deep awareness of the light will be born a balance wherein unconditional love will, in total synergy of spirit, merge with the light to create an awareness of divinity in all things. These two properties of divinity hold the planets in the heavens and the stars in the sky. In reality there is nothing that does not exist without divine love and light. This is what gives matter its form and is what the universe resonates to. Nothing in any dimension of time and space would exist without it.

When we embrace these divine properties and are in perfect harmony and sync within, we have the power and ability to access all the wisdom hidden within the ethers. You tap into this wisdom through meditation, prayer, communion with nature or whatever form of worship you prefer. The method needed to tap into divine wisdom is discovered when we learn to be quiet within and then learn to listen to the inner voice of our higher self. This inner voice then connects us to the almighty I Am presence, our spirit guides, our guardian angels and to God. When we tune into that all-powerful source within we are able to tap into the universal mind and all knowledge and wisdom is then at our fingertips. It is within these parameters then that everything we need for our spiritual evolution is there for the asking.

When we tap into the universal mind we are tapping into what is referred to as the Akashic Records. These records store within them the cause, effect, record and the memory of every soul's existence throughout all time. Every person's thoughts, actions, words and deeds are stored within these records, which are often referred to as the universal filing system. The records of every living being are impressed upon the ethers and are stored within the Akashic Records or what is also called The Book of Knowledge. There are many who believe it is from this primary source of wisdom that the four principles of fire, earth, air and water were created.

The Akashic Records refer to the frequency grid matrix that creates all of our realities at any given moment. The word akashic originated from a Sanskrit word meaning 'sky, space or ether', and is understood to be a collection of mystical knowledge encoded upon the ethers. These records exist upon a higher frequency vibratory matrix and can only be accessed by going within and tuning in to your higher self.

These records are also often referred to as the cosmic or universal mind or as the collective consciousness of all beings .All of these descriptions are correct. There are many who believe that clairvoyants make psychic perception possible when they access these records. Nostradamus claimed to have been able to tap into these records to make his amazing predictions. The renowned psychic of the 1940's, Edgar Cayce, was able to access these records during his readings which were done in a trance-like sleep state. Both of these individuals were able to impart startling revelations of truth and clarity through this process. When you tune into this universal mind through whatever form of meditation works for you, or by simply being quiet and communing with nature, you are tuning into the universal mind of God. All knowledge is then yours for the asking. You can ask your spirit guides, guardian angels or the divine masters to assist you in your spiritual evolution into time and space. It is this evolution that is the goal of every soul. When we, through meditation, raise our vibrations we are able to hear the divine masters. This process is called being clairaudient. Tuning in to the divine realm and the Akashic Records is like tuning in to a radio. At first all you get is static. But then through meditation as your vibrations rise, you begin to hear a very clear melody of knowledge that is there for everyone to access. This knowledge and insight sometimes comes to us in a flash or in a moment of deja' vu, clairaudience or clairvoyance and our world is forever changed. Life then sends us all we need to further us along the pathway to enlightenment. The higher beings residing in the realm of the divine are waiting in the wings to assist us along this road of enchantment. In the recorded history of the Tibetan priesthood there is a saying, 'When the student is ready, the teacher will appear'. This prophecy is totally true. As stated earlier, I have known and experienced it along my own journey of enlightenment and can attest to its truth and reliability. These great teachers in our lives appear sometimes when we least expect them. They come to us when we have a deep and abiding desire to learn, to know and to experience the wisdom of the ages. When our desire to learn and understand the esoteric mysteries is projected out into the ethers true magic occurs. What we most desire we then manifest into our realities and our lives are forever changed. True avatars or spiritually enlightened and evolved teachers appear in our lives to teach us and to help move us forward along the journey to enlightenment. These beings come into our lives when we are ready to receive them. You experience their presence when you open up to learning and have a desire to know and to understand the divine mysteries. As we move forward along the spiritual road of life, we need to pay attention to the messages being sent to us.

These avatars can be seemingly normal individuals who impart magic and knowledge into our lives and in the process turn on the light bulb of illumination so the road before you is totally lighted and your pathway to your spiritual evolution is crystal clear. These avatars show us our true spirituality. They hold up a mirror so we can see our soul reflected back. They help us go within and find our true selves, not the self we thought we were, but rather the self we truly are. These teachers teach us to be aware, to pay attention to the messages around us, to observe all of life and learn from it. They help us essentially to remember what we have always known but have forgotten. They teach us to tune in to the higher frequency of the divine realm through prayer and meditation. Sometimes they simply spark a deeply rooted desire to know and to understand the mysteries of life therefore propelling us forward to do our own research through the books we read, the films we watch and the seminars and lectures we listen to that spark an excitement within us to know and understand more. We are then propelled forward into a whirlwind of knowledge that resonates deeply within our souls. We recognize the truths we are hearing and reading. We embrace these truths and are now on our own quest to learn more and to understand the mysteries of the universe. As we grow in knowledge we then become avatars ourselves to others who are just in the beginning stages of their own quest for universal wisdom and truth. We are then able to tap into our higher self which possesses all wisdom, all truth, all power, and all innocence and impart this knowledge to those who need it. Within the parameters of our free will remember we all have within us the ability to choose whether or not we will tune into our higher self and receive all this power, which has always been our birthright throughout all of our lifetimes.

We as human beings are finally beginning to realize essentially who we really are. We are finally beginning to recognize our magical abilities. We are becoming aware that we are in truth spiritual beings residing within a mundane body; a body that is our temple and our sanctuary. We must all remember who and what we are: magical beings that through a process of amnesia have forgotten our truths and have lost our way.

When we go within and connect to our higher self and to the divine realm, we tap into a well of wisdom and esoteric mysteries that are profound and we begin to understand finally this connection to all of life. We are all connected. We are all one. We are all of the light and the light resonates within us all. We are all one with God in whatever manner of worship you prefer. It is in our quest to become one with God that we open up our minds and begin to see the beauty of the world as it truly is. Many have recognized this reality. Others are still floundering. But we are all on the same journey. We all need to turn on the light of our divine spirituality.

We need to understand that what binds the one, binds us all. The hatred, greed, gluttony, apathy, prejudice, intolerance, anger and insensitivity of our world is not working and will never work. The universe is trying to get us to wake up and pay attention! The vibrations of the world we live in are insisting our lessons be instant. When we act out in a negative, the response from the universe is immediate. There is no waiting to get it right in the next lifetime. We are being clobbered upside the head and admonished by the other side with, "How many times do you need to repeat this lesson before you get it right?" We are all being held accountable for our actions! The universe is commanding us to wake up. All the events in our world are in direct response to our actions. Everything around us, both the discord and the harmony, we all have had a part in creating. The divine realm, for the first time in a millennium, is here at our disposal just for the asking. The two living colors of cobalt blue and violet are there for us to use. They are there for us to heal ourselves and our world. All the tools we need are now at our disposal. To use any of these methods we need to go within in whatever method works for us and ask for help. Ask for help from your guardian angels who were assigned to you at first inception and have been with you throughout all of time. Ask for help from your higher self where all knowledge and wisdom reside. Ask for help from your spirit guides who came into your presence at first breath and are always guiding and assisting you. Ask for help from the Ascended Masters in whatever form of religion you follow. All will answer you. All are waiting in the wings to guide and assist you along your journey. Call upon the Guardian Angels to guard and protect, to heal and enlighten and to open up the pathway to knowledge. As you can see, there are many pathways to take, use the one that feels right to you. When we invoke the help from any one of these sources all are joyful. To invoke something is to command that it occur. It is a call, a claim, a request to come, to be present in an instant of asking. It is the act of summoning whatever it is you are asking for into your presence.

When we call upon the higher realm for help we do so through our heart chakra. This is where these divine beings go to communicate with us. Within our heart chakra we each hold the divine presence of God. God holds up a mirror and we are each reflected back. When God created man in his own image, He created this divine presence within each of our hearts. All of us contain this spark of divinity within.

Hermann Hesse wrote the book "Siddhartha", a wonderfully enlightened story about a Brahmin priest's journey into enlightenment. In this gem of a book Siddhartha states "Within you is a stillness and sanctuary to which you can retreat to at any time and be yourself".

Within each of us there is a sanctuary that resides within our heart center. This heart center is our temple. It is our spiritual spa if you will, it is a place that resides deep within us where we can go to at any time and be renewed. Each of us has this. None are excluded. When we go within we create heaven on earth. Heaven is the place within each of us that dances with the love and light of creation. Heaven resides within our heart centers and resonates within our seat of consciousness. It is all light, all love, and all joy! It is the universal communicator. It is the energy of creation. It is the face of God. It reflects back to us our humanity and it is within this humanity we will then know and recognize our divinity. There is divinity in everything. There is divine resonance, light and love in all matter. Spirit dances to the love and light of creation. Spirit dances and resonates to divine love and to God. Spirit exists in every corner of the universe. Spirit, divine love and divine light are all one. It is all there is. It is the I Am presence and is reflected within all of us along our journey through ourselves that each of us takes on the road to enlightenment .At the end of this journey we emerge on the other side into the brilliance of divine love and light. When we finally embrace our divinity we are bathed in a new reality of one energy, one perception and we realize in that one instant there is divinity in all things. We realize God is in the center of consciousness of all beings and we are all one, we are all connected, we are all dancing with the spirit of divine creation.

CHAPTER 9

THE CENTRAL SUN OF CREATION

"In the dark dreary nights, when the storm is at its most fierce, the lighthouse burns bright so the sailors can find their way home again. In life the same light burns. This light is fueled with love, faith and hope. And through life's most fierce storms these three burn their brightest so we can find our way home again."

- unknown -

All of life coalesces around the Central Sun. This sun sustains the life of the universe. It is within this infinite universe all of the powers of creation exist in harmony one to the other. All exist in a complete synergy of love and light. All exist within the Alpha and the Omega who are the twin flames of the cosmic ascended Christ consciousness. The Alpha and Omega balance the masculine and feminine polarity of God within the infinite cosmos of the Central Sun, which is a vortex of spiritual and physical energy vibrating within every cell, atom and molecule of humanity and of all existing life forms. The Central Sun is the center of the universe. It is the center of the cosmos and is the point of integration of spirit and matter wherein spirit merges with matter to give life to the universe. Matter then transcends once again to return to spirit. The interchangeability of matter and spirit, as so profoundly stated by Congressman Dennis Kucinich from Ohio, "...means the starlit magic of the outmost life of the universe becomes the soul light magic of the innermost life of our self". It is the point of origin of all physical and spiritual creations.

The great star Sirius is said to be the focus of the central sun in our galaxy. The Central Sun holds the splendor of the cosmic Christ within its heart and radiates this Christ consciousness out to all of creation. It is this radiation of the love and light from the cosmic Christ of the Central Sun that gives life to all; where the inanimate becomes animate and all spiritual worlds are therein draped with physicality. This Central Sun permeates each soul and is interconnected an intertwined with the seven seats of consciousness, the seven chakras and the four body systems existing within every man. The Central Sun is sometimes referred to as the "Sun of Righteousness" and can, when called upon or invoked, heal the mind and body in a synchronistic union from within and without. This Central Sun is known as the light of God that resides within us all.

Within this Central Sun reside all of the realms of creation. Da Vid in his essay on 'Astrological Events Indicate the Future is Now' states, "We are all living within a multidimensional holographic universe, where all is energy, all is light, and all is consciousness. Indeed the ancient and eternal wisdom has come of age. As we become progressively aware of the fact that we are living in an organic, multidimensional, expanding "Yes Universe", we are given the unprecedented opportunity to transform our lives in accordance with the understanding that we live in an infinitely abundant, benevolent and super intelligent universe governed by the law of love".

Within this Central Sun resides the angelic realm. The Angels who reside within this realm are beings of love and light and are governed by the law of love. Their sole purpose is to serve God and enlighten and integrate all of humanity into the love and light of this eternal wisdom. The Angels represent the nurturing and feminine aspects of God and act on His behalf as spiritual protectors, healers, messengers and guides of all creation. As such they represent all aspects of life from the mundane to the profound.

The Archangels are a much more advanced level of angelic evolution. They are the highest rank in the hierarchy of the angelic realm. These Angels stand before God and are sent by God as his messengers to transmit to all the living light of the "I Am that I Am" which is the individualized presence of the God focus for each individual soul. As such each of these Archangels bears the weight of the God presence within their beings and each are a direct representative of the divine synergy of the love and light of creation.

Our beautiful planet is comprised of many interconnected and multidimensional realms that comprise the mundane world. Within this matrix reside the four kingdoms of nature. These kingdoms are the mineral, plant, animal and human kingdoms. Of these four kingdoms, the human kingdom is the only one classified in a totally separate category due to the fact the human kingdom is the only kingdom blessed with the gift of free will. All of the other kingdoms are guarded, protected and watched over by a group of angelic beings known as "Devas". Devas serve the elemental forces of nature. The word Deva comes from Sanskrit and means "intelligent beings". Every flower, plant, tree, river and mountain has an angelic being that is the caretaker, if you will, for that particular seat of consciousness. All of life forms have a consciousness that co-exist one to the other in tandem. Each of these forms of consciousness represented within the different kingdoms sustains and nourishes the life force within that particular kingdom as well as the life force existing within all the other kingdoms. Nature holds up a mirror so we can see and feel this amazing and astonishing interconnectedness of all life. There is an order and respect that prevails within these kingdoms. It is that same order and respect we all need to incorporate into our own lives. We as the human race are caretakers to the other three kingdoms due to our gift of free will. We are also the only life force on this planet that can eradicate the life form of another through our negativity of spirit. We are the only beings that kill each other simply because the other person does not share and hold our point of view both as an individual and as a nation. We need to stop killing and abusing each other and remember we are all interconnected. We need to have a reverence for all life because when we are irreverent nothing in life is sacred and we lose our sense of being connected to all of life and we are then lost. When we are irreverent our abuse of each other and the other kingdoms is profound. When we are irreverent we defile the earth for our own gain and profit, we destroy plants and trees to sustain our greed and we abuse and kill the animals that are in our care. We have forgotten we are the caretakers of these other kingdoms. We have forgotten our connection to spirit and to each other. We have lost sight of the fact the earth we defile sustains our life and that the plants and forests we decimate all in the name of profit, provide the very air that we breathe. We have also lost sight of the fact that the animals in our care are a direct reflection of the unconditional love of God. They unilaterally give us unconditional love and in return all they ask is that we nurture, protect and love them. All they ask of us is to mirror into our own lives the unconditional love that is reflected in their eyes. They are our connection to the Creator and to the infinite love, wisdom and light of the universe. They are the direct reflection of the heart of God. Is it any wonder that 'dog' is God spelled backwards? Our beloved animals are a gift that was given to us so we could reconnect within the heart of our beings and remember that unconditional love is the most powerful of forces and reflect that power back into our own lives. When we abuse, decimate, torture and kill those life forms entrusted into our care, the heart of God weeps for we have forgotten our divinity and have forgotten we are all one, we are all connected in mind, body and spirit. We then turn our backs on the light and have truly lost our way. When this happens we become one with the darkness and deny within ourselves our spark of divinity that resides within, and then the extreme manifestation of the negative ego in its most vicious and negative form takes over. It is our mission to shine the light of unconditional love for all to see. We are all caretakers of our world. It is the responsibility of each of us to nurture and protect those in our care. As a human race it is our responsibility both as an individual and as a nation to lift up the consciousness of those who are downtrodden and abused. It is our responsibility to all the generations to come to nurture and protect our children for they are the very foundation that our society is built upon. We need to stop abusing the innocent in our world. When we abuse our children we begin to destroy their spirit. We begin to destroy their hope and an entire generation is lost. It is imperative we lift our children up into the light of unconditional love. It is a proven fact that if a baby is ignored and not cuddled, cherished and shown love, that baby's spirit will shrivel up and die. That baby will become listless and soon will simply cease to exist.

It is our responsibility to stop the atrocities occurring out of our lack of reverence and our supreme ignorance. We need to remember our roles of protectors, providers and leaders and begin to acknowledge what we have done, what we are doing and stop the nonsense. Our children are our greatest legacy. They are our gifts to each other and to the world. We need to raise them in the light of understanding and unconditional love. We need to stop passing on to our children this sense of entitlement. The only entitlement any of us has is of unconditional love and respect for each other. No one is better than the other. Everyone is perfect even within their imagined imperfections. This is what makes us all unique. We are all important and deserving of all of the gifts of life. Each and every one of us is a brick in the foundation of the reality of the whole. Each of these bricks is totally necessary for the strength of the whole. When any one of these bricks is destroyed or ignored, therefore left to deteriorate, the entire foundation crumbles. Our foundation needs to be shored up and supported by all or the reality of what we have collectively created will crumble. Now, some of that reality needs to be put to rest because it concentrates only on the negative. We need to begin to reject all of the negative rhetoric we have been subjected to by our government, the media and by the world we live in and by each other. We all need to look in the mirror and accept our own part in this web of negativity that has embraced our planet. It is a web of our own making and it will take all of us individually and collectively to remain in the present and to visualize a better world. Once we visualize a better world we have the makings of the blueprint that will instigate change and the universal mind will then send us everything we need to open up our eyes and take responsibility for the world we have created. We are not being careful and in our carelessness to our world, our environment and to each other we are in danger of destroying the very foundation our world was built upon.

When are we going to learn to be humane? When are we going to realize just how connected we all are? For example, when the media reports a catastrophe or tells about a 'breaking story' and puts a negative spin upon it, all who are watching are then bathed in this negativity. The media needs to be much more careful as these negative thoughts become our reality. We buy into the negativity being reported and because the 'respected' beings who comprise our news networks are the ones telling us these supposed truths many assume everything being reported is true. When did we stop reporting the news as it is and begin to integrate personal opinion into the reporting? And when did that personal opinion become so important we felt the need to control our viewer's point of view? Accountability is now upon us. What we reap we are now in a very dramatic way sewing. When are we going to learn as a global community that the universal laws of cause and effect are exact? The laws of karma don't differentiate. They are unbiased and affect everyone and every nation. Due to our supreme obtuseness as a civilization we are in danger of destroying ourselves. Wake up! Pay attention! We share a responsibility and are each accountable for the mess of our financial markets, of our governments and also most important of all, of the chaos and mess that our planet is currently going through. We need to picture the world as it should be. If we want stabilization we need to collectively visualize it. Once we do this the blueprint will follow. We can change our economy simply by believing we can. That my friends is the most important first step. Stop buying into all the negativity and begin to visualize a better way. Soon that better way will open up before you and the solutions to the changes you have been searching for will appear. It is that simple. Sometimes the truths we search for hide in plain sight.

Look at the world and visualize the world as you want it to be. See the possibilities for that change and begin to visualize a new blueprint with new and improved eyes. Pay attention. Be present because the universe will send you the tools to implement that change. If you are not aware and paying attention it could pass you by. See the world as you want it to be and go and create a new reality of hope, unconditional love and understanding with a reverence for all life. Be accountable for the world you are constantly creating by the thoughts you have. Make your choices be of peace rather than of destruction. Pave the way for a new world order. Take your power back that you have abdicated to those who you have mistakenly given your trust to. Trust in the power of yourself. Trust in the power of your mind to visualize and recreate your existing reality. Imagine how that would feel. Imagine how the world would look with your new vision and then go and create it. Be the builder, contractor and foreman of your own thoughts and beliefs. You have this power within you. Use it. Demand to be heard. Become the advocate for change! Move into your higher self and become one with all. Feel the connection. Believe in hope. Believe in change. Believe in yourself. Change is a good thing. It keeps our world from becoming stagnant. Ironically change is the only constant concept that propels us forward. Embrace this change both from within yourself and from within your world. Honor it. Move into and become one with it. Believe in yourselves. You are all divine beings who are extremely powerful. Embrace that power. Believe in it. It is like a sleeping giant that once awakened will redefine the world you live in. Once awakened this inner power can move mountains and bring about change and reform quicker than anything else ever could. Use this power for good. Use it to re-establish order in a world gone mad. Believe that you can and march forward into this whirlwind of change we are all currently experiencing on our planet. Make a difference. We are now at a turning point in our evolution of spirit. Our future is being created now in the choices we are making. We are currently experiencing a progressive transformation of consciousness both within our government and within our world. It is this transformation of consciousness that will ultimately set us free. We are awakening to a new world order of love, light and wisdom. Everywhere we look transformation is occurring on every level. It is like the world has been tossed asunder and when it rights, hopefully, a new and improved world order will define us all. The key to our transformation of consciousness lies in our ability to grasp and understand the complete synergy of love and light wherein we have a remembrance that we are all of a collective whole, one with the universe in endless creative energy, multidimensional, where all that is resonates in love, light and wisdom.

Deborah Fields

CHAPTER 10

THE ETERNAL NOW

"A brief candle; both ends burning

An endless mile; a bus wheel turning

A friend to share the lonesome times

A handshake and a sip of wine.

So say it loud and let it ring

We are all a part of everything

The future, present and the past

Fly on proud bird

You're free at last.

\- Charlie Daniels -

The supreme moment of now is the state of being that all beings should come from. Nothing exists except the now. Past, present and future all exist simultaneously in the now. It is a state of being that keeps us all present in life, in the moment and allows us to access the knowledge and wisdom of the ages much more profoundly.

Everything in the cosmos revolves around the eternal now and exists as one. All of life revolves around the Supreme God Source, the Alpha and the Omega, the I Am that I Am. This God Source of the Central Sun is quite simply the energy that fuels the universe. Without it there would be no life, no light; only a vast unending void. Within the now of God's universe exists the equation of divine polarity, of the Alpha and the Omega, the masculine and feminine counterparts to our beings, of the plus and minus of creation. Our own spiritual development requires us to balance this polarity within so that we can then express both power and love within the unification of God.

Within all of life there are polar opposites. Within every life form there is a positive/negative polarity that exists to bring balance. It is this balance that is needed to sustain and maintain life itself. Nothing in the universe would exist if this principle were not in place.

In the beginning there was the 'word', and the word of God brought forth this divine polarity that is ever present within all of life in any time frame, in any universe, both known or unknown.

This polarity dances within the light and sound of creation and is what gives balance to everything in God's infinite Omniverse. For example, the antithesis of light would be darkness, of love would be hatred, of good would be evil, of beautiful would be ugly, of harmony would be disharmony, and of peace would be chaos. I'm sure by now you get the point. Even our planet bears the polarities of the north and south poles.

The divine attributes of love, wisdom, and will work in complete synergy with the light and sound of creation to bring harmony and balance to all. In 'Saint Germain on Alchemy, Formulas for Spiritual Transformation' written by Mark and Elizabeth Clare Prophet, they write, "In the original premise of the Godhead, power or the will to be, is the thesis...wisdom is the antithesis and love is the synthesis...This true synthesis of the divine attributes reveals that love, wisdom and power are in reality the one indivisible/undivided whole which can never be divided or divisive. Their atoms chanting as they chart the spheres: we are one, we are one, we are one."

Each of us needs to embrace this polarity within ourselves in a complete synergy of love and light. Each of us is a perfect balance of both the light and the dark, of good and evil, of beautiful and ugly and of perfection ad imperfection, just to name a few. The dualities of life are endless and all encompassing. These polarities bring balance and harmony to our lives and when in perfect balance reflect the God-self within. Each is counter balanced by its exact polar opposite in order to hold up the mirror to us and reflect back our divinity.

We are each given the choice to either embrace the light or to embrace the darkness along the road in our quest for spiritual illumination. If you had never experience the blackest of nights how then would you be able to recognize the moment when you were presented with the perfect of dawn's? If you had never experienced true hatred, bigotry, prejudice and ugliness in humanity, how would you then be able to recognize and then rejoice when you were presented with pure love, tolerance, compassion and beauty in the world? Both polarities exist to teach us and move us forward along the road to enlightenment.

All of the hatred being expressed all over our beautiful planet is being balanced by the love and light pouring out of the hearts of the lightbearers. This language of love and light is reflected within the very essence of our beings and is the tool through which we communicate with the Divine Intelligence through the perfection of the frequency of love. As we awaken in our evolution of spirit we will begin to expand our awareness and begin to forge a bridge to the divine realm. We will begin to communicate with this higher dimension of lightbearers who come to us bearing the truth and light of creation. The white Christ light radiates from their beings as they hold within them the frequency of light and information for the world. They are the Ascended Masters and teachers of the world and are truly enlightened beings made up of pure light and consciousness who are one with all that is. They are the all powerful, all loving, all knowing, all seeing, omnipresent God force. They are part of a spiritual organization called the 'Great White Brotherhood' united for the highest purpose of God in man; united to bring about the spiritual evolution of our world.

This is a spiritual order that has ascended from every culture, religion, nationality and gender. It encompasses great beings of light such as; Mother Mary, Jesus the Cosmic Ascended Christ, Moses, Enoch, Mohammed, Elijah, Abraham, Gautama Buddha, Hari, Satyasena, Krishna, Isaiah, Amen- Ptah, Metatron, Melchizedek, Saint Germain, Lord Maitreya, Omri-Tos, Lanello, Maha Chohan, Djwal Khul and members of the heavenly hosts who are the spiritual hierarchy directly concerned with the evolution of our world. There are 144,000 Ascended masters that comprise the Great White Brotherhood. This Brotherhood of Light is under the direction of the Brotherhood of Micheal, the Brotherhood of Enoch, and the Brotherhood of Melchizedek, which direct the seventy Brotherhoods of the Great White Brotherhood. These brotherhoods serve as a field of intelligence and Divine Light who assist the Father in repairing the Universes so that all can evolve into the infinite wisdom and glory of God. They have transcended the cycles of karma and rebirth and reside within the hierarchy of God.

The main purpose of the Great White Brotherhood is to help us ascend back into the light and to help us open up our channel so we are all once again in direct communication with whatever our concept of God is. They are here and present at this time on our planet to empower us and to move us forward along the road in our evolution of spirit.

We are all on some level bearers of the light. Our pathways are as different and unique as we are. Yet these pathways are all heading in the same direction. We are evolving at our own individual pace within our own spiritual transformation in our collective expansion into the consciousness of love and light. It is this expansion of consciousness that defines us. Each person's place along the road in their spiritual evolution back into the light of divinity is protected by the divine law stating that those beings of lesser awareness will not be given more choice or more responsibility than they are able to handle. And that their manifested reality will be within the parameters of a level of consciousness that is compatible with where they stand in life.

Life is often likened to a schoolroom wherein the lessons of life are best learned upon the earth plane of existence which is after all our classroom where we obtain divine knowledge. It is within this classroom that we grow and evolve by degrees according to whatever level we are currently in. You will never be given more than you can handle at any given moment. You needn't have fear of the learning process as one does not jump from kindergarten into high school in the blink of an eye. The process of moving into the love and light of divinity is a gradual expansion of consciousness. If the consciousness of the individual has only reached the level of a blade of grass then that is their level of comfort and there is nothing wrong with that state of being. However, as our consciousness gradually expands we then become aware of being more than we thought we were, and we begin to see ourselves as just one small part of a vast and expansive whole. As our consciousness expands into the light of knowledge it can never contract back into the abyss of ignorance. One of the universal laws states that once there is expansion of spirit there can not be contraction. Once we expand into the light of awareness and knowledge we move out of the darkness of ignorance and apathy and true illumination of spirit occurs. We move into the light and become one with whatever our concept of God is. We begin to radiate the light from within and in so doing we then illuminate the path both for ourselves and for others to follow. 'We' become lightbearers ourselves, as the word lightbearer means to bear the light.

The sole purpose of those who have ascended into the order of the Great White Brotherhood is the embracement of the motto, "I am my brother's keeper". These highly evolved beings are the heralders of peace. They collectively hold the frequency of light and divinity for the world and into the darkness they are marching forth from every corner of the universe to enlighten, to teach and to heal the wounds of humanity.

We are living within a vortex of great change; a changing of vibration that for some will be very unsettling and very unnerving. Due to this a great fear has been embraced that is so unnecessary. This change is upon us whether we embrace it or reject it. The darkness is pushing against the light in an effort to conquer and control. But make no mistake. The light of the divine will of God will always overcome the darkness.

We are being presented in a very real and concrete way with these very principles. We are mired in a government that has forgotten its purpose and has lost its way. A government that believes that violence and war are inevitable, that is constantly bombarding us through the willing puppetry of the media of the possibility of terrorist's attacks against our nation, of possible deployment of nuclear warheads against the world, of a failing domestic and global economy and of catastrophic global climate changes. All are presented in such a way as to instigate a deep-rooted fear within us thereby sanctifying the unthinkable. Within the chaos of this matrix we find the world we once knew and were comfortable with, changing and shifting before our very eyes. What was up is down. What was once right is now wrong and as the parameters of our world shift, a new world order is about to begin.

The dark forces afoot are becoming more brazen in their attempts to conquer and control. Thus the legions of light known as the Great White Brotherhood have descended among us and are quietly and steadily helping mankind evolve. In so doing they are lifting us out of the abyss of ignorance.

When the legions of lightbearers take action to preserve the harmony of the world, they will do so peacefully without any loss of life. They will not allow nuclear war as a tool to destroy and are working tirelessly and effortlessly towards peaceful resolutions. They have stated emphatically, that mankind will not be allowed to take the evil thoughts of war, violence and weapons of destruction into space! They have told us to heed this statement and to heed it well as our future existence hangs in the balance. They will not allow negativity around the Central Sun of the universe.

These beings are teaching us that what we reap, we sow. What we visualize we create. In our constant bombardment of negativity we have embraced the negative and have collectively created the negative scenarios we are now being forced to deal with .We must rise above the negativity that our planet has been bombarded with. We need to learn to transmute these negative thought patterns into patterns of hope. We need to visualize our world as ever expanding and beautiful, full of abundance for all of humanity. We need to reject all the negativity we are being brainwashed into believing and begin to see the truth of love and light and of hope and redemption that is ever prevalent in all of life.

This has been a time of intense clearing and cleansing of the negative forces we have been subjected to whether we were aware of them or not. This is a time of healing and purification. Within the parameters of this purification process we have been subjected to over the last decades, we have steadily been overcoming these lower vibrations on earth. Many portals are now opening all over the world and are bathing us in new energies of love and light. The Great White Brotherhood is using the tools of love and light from the divine realm and is working to bring about a massive healing and peace for our planet.

Over the last decade our governments have all seeded the way for global change. The world is now hungry for a new world directive, for a new world order. Business as usual is no longer accepted or wanted. New matrixes are being created out of the chaos that our greed and ignorance have caused .There is now the hope that these new matrixes will pave the way for a new world order of respect, tolerance, happiness, fulfillment, abundance and a peaceful co-existence for all humanity. Wherein all of humanity will then expand into the light of awareness and knowledge and move out of the darkness of greed, ignorance and apathy. When this occurs, true global illumination will descend upon us.

Governments all over the world are now being forced to reassess and clarify what they stand for. They are now being required to be accountable for their actions. A mirror is being held up and all the atrocities are being reflected back for us to see. Transformation is upon us. How we choose to embrace this transformation will be every man, woman and child's goal. It will be our free will and our choices that will ultimately define us. Choose wisely. The pathway before you will either illuminate or will distort the process. In the end each of us stands alone. Each of us must make the ultimate choice to embrace or to reject. That is our supreme gift from the divine realm. It is up to us to heal the world we live in and to bring about global peace upon this planet we all call home.

Deborah Fields

Chapter 11

THE QUICKENING

"Your hopes dreams and aspirations are legitimate. They are trying to take you airborne, above the clouds, above the storms, if you only let them."

-William James-

The quickening is the beginning of the evolution of our expansion of consciousness both as an individual and as a collective whole. We are all now at this moment in time being forced to be accountable for our actions. Whether or not those actions were born from the greed of the individual or from the obtuseness and ignorance of our own governments, all are now being held fully accountable. We are now mired in the muck of our own creation and it is up to all of us to pull ourselves out of this abyss we have currently found ourselves teetering upon. It will be up to all of us to help heal the open wounds of the world. All of the atrocities have got to stop. We need to replace greed with the knowledge of abundance for all. We need to stop the hoarding of the wealth of the few at the expense of the wealth for the many.

A spiritual quickening is taking place all over the world inspiring an interconnectedness of spirit amongst those who are aware of the accelerated vibratory harmonics that are occurring now at this time on our planet. This interconnectedness of spirit bridges all faiths, all nationalities and all genders. It emphasizes the reality of oneness, of being totally connected. When one hand bleeds we all bleed. The disintegration of our financial markets is a prime example of this principle in action. We are all bleeding as a result of this. Yet, in the near future due to the results of all of this chaos and cleansing a much stronger financial market will be born. This new and improved financial market will be much more balanced and will be based on the reality of free and unbiased enterprise that embraces the masses rather than the select few.

This cleansing is happening on a global scale in part because what affects one affects us all, and also to hold up the mirror of life and to reflect back to all the reality of what we have each had a hand in creating. What we visualize as an individual we then create as a collective group. When one cancerous thought contaminates the whole, the collectiveness of the whole begins to sicken. Negativity contains within it the seeds of our very destruction. We have been bombarded with an onslaught of negative broadcasting, of negative articles in newspapers and magazines and of all the negative realities which we have all collectively brought into being. What you experience is directly related to what your belief structure is. The world and reality you live in is in direct proportion to what you have mentally created both the negative aspects as well as the positive ones.

Yet this duality of life, meaning the duality of opposites, where we pit one side against the other, is also the yellow brick road that can lead us all towards universal truths. This reality we are experiencing is not our prison but is rather our schoolroom. It is through the lessons we are currently learning that we will find unity. It is through the lesson of duality that we will clearly see the promise of this unification. The Unification of our socio-economic structure, our monetary economic matrix and our geopolitical positions hopefully will be the end result of the lessons learned.

All of the negativity we are currently experiencing is a direct result of fear. Fear of the lack of abundance causes greed and greed was the monkey wrench that was thrown into the economic matrix of our system. It ultimately caused the deterioration and disintegration we are currently experiencing. We need to look solidly at our fears and ask ourselves why we are holding these destructive thought patterns. We need to begin replacing these with positive thought patterns therefore changing the matrix of our realities. Learn to go within and listen to your fears. What are these fears? Define them, face them and then challenge them. Move through them and come out on the other side with renewed eyes of awareness and understanding. When you do this you'll realize fear is nothing more than an inflated bubble that when popped becomes a lot of nothing but hot air. Life is a schoolroom that enables us to learn the duality between hope and fear. Through example it teaches us to go within and embrace our own power. When we come from a point of inner power we can perform miracles. Fear is a teaching emotion. It enables us to really look at ourselves, to go within and examine who we are. Who do we want to be? It is the antithesis of hope. We move through one to get to the other. When we move through our fears into hope we move into an empowerment of being. We move into an inner empowerment that then totally alters the reality of our own lives in a shift of consciousness which then in turn opens us up and connects us to all universal truths.

We need to stop being the victim and take back our power. True power is "never" about having power and control over another. Rather it is about being able to stand alone within our empowerment of spirit; to move into ourselves into who we are, to embrace this powerful being from within and to become peaceful warriors who uplift the whole rather than destroy it.

Within us resides the wisdom of all universal truths. This wisdom within does not conform to linear thought patterns and is all knowing. It is up to each and every one of us to free our minds from the boundaries of linear thinking and to move out of the box of comfort that we have created. We need to move into the realm of power that comes to each of us when we embrace our true selves. True power comes to us when we are living in the now of creation and are present within the moment. When we are present and aware within the moment of "now" great wisdom then becomes apparent. To be present in the " now " is to not worry about the past or fret about the future but to experience life to its fullest, moment to moment, second to second, and to grasp every single pleasure as it is being presented to you.

Your mind is capable of amazing feats. It has the power to instantly manifest your reality at any given moment. With the embracement of either positive or negative thoughts the mind has the power to change that reality with a flip of a switch. It has the power to change your thought patterns into a new reality of being, therefore manifesting a new matrix of light, sound and total unconditional love for the amazing beings that you are always in the process of becoming. Remember that within every shadow and dark pocket we have created within our realm of thinking is brilliant light that stands behind all illusion. All negativity is an illusion that brings us closer to the truth. Your mind uses these illusions of negativity through the vehicle of your fears to open up the doorway to your true reality of being. The mind uses your experience within the world you live in to make you feel safe and secure. It is this mechanism that gives us comfort and gives us safe boundaries of existence. The mind brings you great capacity to make sense of what you are experiencing in the now. It is the doorway through which you view your world. However, it can only take you so far. Once you reach its limitations it is up to you to make a leap of faith and to make the journey into the unknown. The mind will then take you on a journey of unlimited truth as it holds within itself the capacity to exist beyond limited thinking, beyond human restrictions and beyond time and space into the eternal wisdom of now. It will then open the window to your soul and reflect back to all who dare to look an amazing new vista of magic and wonder.

We are living in the illusion of our own creation. It is within this supreme illusion, that we are stuck within the boundaries of our own making which has caused us all such unnecessary pain and suffering. Once we grasp the truth that all of life is an illusion that can change on a dime through the power of our thought patterns much like the kaleidoscope changes when turned and that each thought pattern has the potential to bring us all equal amounts of both happiness and unmitigated joy as well as unbelievable sorrow and pain, then and only then will the unlimited expansive beauty of our world open up before us. All of a sudden there are now infinite possibilities and infinite choices to be made. We are not ever stuck within a situation. Sometimes all it takes is a change of attitude that makes all the difference in how we view the world. Other times it requires a change in direction ever so slightly to open up new horizons that will then bring us great peace of mind and joy of spirit .Remember fear is only a teacher and holds within itself perfect love, wisdom and hope.

Fear has unleashed upon our planet all of its poisons: poisons like cancer, Aids, poverty, hunger, nuclear war, torture, terrorism and genocide. These are just some of the faces of fear. Yet, through it all throughout all of time humanity has constantly sought to know love and this is then the pathway to truth and transformation. This is our pathway to self-actualization and a quickening of spirit. This is our pathway home.

Fear is the voice that tells you it wants you to *feel* safe and secure. Love is the voice telling you that you *are* safe and secure. Learn to love yourself unconditionally. Learn to know who you are and what it is you stand for. Learn to understand what it is you believe in. Move into these phases of being and when you do you'll experience a quickening of being and an excitement that comes when you are walking upon your true pathway.

Open up to unconditional love and embrace the power from within. Learn to face your fears, challenge them and move through them into the hope and promise of a new tomorrow. Become the change you imagine and create a better world.

.

Chapter 12

THE LIGHTBEARER'S

"It is my choice – either to be satisfied with a drop or to seek the almighty ocean."

- Sri Chinmoy -

The need for change upon our beautiful planet has never been more apparent than it is today. This need for change can be found in both the mundane as well as in the profound. All of humanity co-exists in this one moment in time in order to facilitate this change. From the evil of the world to the incredible good that can be found in the world, we are all marching forward towards this change. This change is one of perception in how we not only see the world but in how we interact within the world in which we live. It is imperative we take off our blinders of fear and begin to see life as it truly is. All of life is held within total perfection even the part of life that we deem evil. After all, evil is simply live spelled backwards. Evil is darkness. It is the absence of light and all of darkness is a disturbance of the light of creation. It is all about duality. It is all about perception. Evil only exists if you perceive it to be so. Evil, darkness and fear only have power if you give them power. They only have power if you turn away from the light.

The souls who have turned away from the light and have embraced the darkness are souls who have lost their way. They are all at some level seeking redemption. Redemption of mind, body and of spirit. These lost souls have forgotten their divinity. They are the true casualties of our misconceptions and of our warped perceptions. They are the real casualties of us not remembering who we are and where we came from.

These souls need our outpouring of love, compassion and understanding. They are all over the planet and are from every walk of life. They practice every religion known to mankind and embrace every race. They are not gender specific. Within their ranks there are no separations between poverty and wealth as they are contained within each.

This darkness we perceive within is only an illusion. It is only a shadow we have created in our turning our backs upon our own divinity, upon our own spark of creation, upon the light we each carry within us. We are each and every one of us beings of light and are all in the process of embracing and expanding our consciousness. When we collectively express an outpouring of love, compassion and understanding towards are fellow man we begin to uplift the vibrations of the ones who are mired in darkness. We then begin to create an awakening within. All that is needed for this awakening to begin is for each of us to shine the light of divinity into the darkest recesses of the soul and bring about illumination. Through this process we will then bring enlightenment to those souls crying out for help. When we do this we will light the way for others to follow.

As we begin to shine the light of illumination into the darkness we begin to teach those who are lost a new truth and slowly bring them out of the state of ignorance they are entangled in. When we do this we ourselves then become the lightbearers, we become the truthbearers. These lightbearers know instinctively who they are.

They will be drawn to help and to serve humanity at this incredible time on our planet. This is the time of the quickening of the illumination of spirit from within.

These lightbearers will be found everywhere and will come from every walk of life. They will come from the man who shines your shoes to the woman who styles your hair. They will come from the followers of life to the leaders, from the downtrodden to the powerful. These lightbearers of humanity will form an alliance with the Great White Brotherhood and will come from every direction on the planet. They will collectively shine forth the beacon of light and love and begin to heal the rift upon this beautiful planet we are lucky enough to call home. They will begin to heal the open wounds of the world and begin to repair all of the damage we have caused upon Mother Earth through our greed, arrogance, ignorance, apathy and negligence of being.

It will become apparent soon that this change is occurring. Hollywood will be behind this movement helping it gain momentum. Other movements will soon follow. Greenpeace is one of these movements created to facilitate this change. This movement was created to bring about awareness to all of us, that we cannot continue to dishonor our planet and we cannot continue to take our planet and its abundance of natural resources for granted. We have to wake up and begin to behave honorably. We need to find ways to recycle our waste and then use it for the good of all humanity. There are those out there that are doing just this and it will become more prevalent in the years to come. It will be incredibly exciting and uplifting to see how we begin to cleanse this beautiful planet. Whole species have disappeared through our negligence and while new species are being created every day, there is a profound sadness in the loss of these life forms. These lost life forms now exist in a separate realm, in a separate reality. They are waiting for the time when all is in perfect balance again and will then return to our world. They will then once again grace us with their diversity and beauty.

It is up to all of us to bring about this balance that is so needed upon our planet and to believe in the possibilities and the promise of this change. We need to believe in the power of the 'I Am' presence and remember we are all connected. When one has a contamination of spirit we all suffer. When one falls into the pits of despair and is swallowed by the darkness there is a dimming of the light for us all. We need to be aware of our connection and of our interconnection to all of life.

This spiritual connection is ever prevalent in nature and in the earth we live upon. When we dishonor the earth through our collective contamination of the waters we drink and the very air that we breathe we all suffer. When we destroy and decimate an entire forest all in the name of free enterprise, not only do we destroy our trees that give us oxygen but we eliminate entire life forms which then cease to exist. Their loss is our profound loss.

When are we going to take responsibility for our actions? There needs to be accountability here! When are we going to remember that we exist and co-exist in perfect harmony one to the other? Without one, the other does not exist. When are we going to realize when we destroy the earth we are destroying ourselves as well? Mother Earth is a living breathing entity and she will only tolerate so much abuse, indifference and irresponsibility towards her. She will chew us up and spit us out and in the end will cleanse and renew herself and destroy us all in the process.

We need to begin to honor her. This can begin in the smallest of offering by the simple planting of a single flower or blade of grass. When we give back to the earth we are insuring our own longevity of being. We need to embrace and begin this journey. We need to see the possibility and promise of the journey. When we decimate the earth we are breaking our covenant with her. When mankind disobeys cosmic law and exhibits a gathering destructiveness upon the earth, Mother Earth then rebels and removes the problem. We need to begin to mend the rift and to begin to bring balance back into our world. Through our irreverence of Mother Earth we have destroyed entire rainforests throughout our world. By divine law if we destroy one tree, one flower, or one blade of grass we incur negative karma, both as an individual and as a collective whole. When we destroy a tree, plant another one for it is not just the tree that was destroyed. In the process we have also destroyed the natural habitat of entire species of insects, birds and animals that rely upon the forest for their very existence. As with the duality of life the destruction of one destroys the other. We are responsible for the wellbeing of our planet and we are failing miserably at this task.

Now all it takes to reverse this process is to first acknowledge our part in its destruction and to then begin to do something to correct it .We have to move from the point where we have this fear of the lack of abundance into the truth of abundance for all. When we move out of this paralyzing fear and shed it as a snake sheds its skin, we then move into the wisdom of interconnectedness and into our own power of being. When we do we will then come from a point of harmony rather than disharmony. True awareness will then dawn upon us. The sunlight of awareness will then dissipate the mist that has shrouded us in our ignorance and a clearness of vision will then occur.

Honor your world and your world will honor you. Honor yourself and you will then honor your world. Be aware. Conserve where you can. Create new resources that will honor the environment. We will have in our future new resources of alternative fuels and clean energies. These will be born upon this planet in the form of thoughts and ideas directly channeled from the divine realm and the Ascended Masters. These new resources will bring about a shift in the consciousness of our planet to one of inclusion rather than exclusion. These resources will bring about exciting new ideas and will help accelerate the quickening of all humanity.

It will be hard for many to make this change, to make the leap from one to the other. Some will fight it viciously with no thought to the whole of humanity, with only thoughts of self. These beings will either be given the choice to move ahead or they will be left behind. There are many who will instigate these changes and who will embrace this new direction. They will help lead humanity into this new phase of being, into this new millennium of peace, joy and abundance for all .This movement is even now in motion. There are many who are involved in this process at every level. There are many who are now helping to illuminate mankind to the perils of our planet. They are bringing knowledge and understanding through documentaries, books, News programs and special reports and are showing the world the unparalleled dangers we have created through our ignorance, apathy, and arrogance of being.

Many have now taken up this torch of illumination. Many more will follow. We must all help to save the planet. This can begin in the simplest of places such as your local grocery stores where we are given the choice to purchase a reusable grocery bag rather than using paper or plastic. Paper and plastic both decimate and contaminate our environment. Trade Joe's, Whole Foods and other environmentally conscious food stores all sell reusable grocery bags to help preserve the environment. How simple and yet how perfect this is. Many businesses will follow. The movement has begun and there will be no stopping it. We do not have a choice in this if we are to begin the process of saving our planet. We need to fix our environment or we will not be able to survive within it. We all have to heal our world.

It is way beyond the point where we can bury our heads in the sand and pretend all is right with the world. The ostrich method does not work! We need to be responsible consumers. We need to be responsible human beings. We need to honor our world. We need to honor each other and we need to honor ourselves. We need to believe in the possibility of change and the hope for a better tomorrow.

There is a grassroots awakening that is taking place all over this planet. The majority of people who live upon this Planet genuinely care about other people and the wellbeing of Mother Earth. The movement to go green is upon us. Most people want to live within a lifestyle that not only enables them to embrace their hopes and dreams but also honors the earth as well. Most of us are yearning for a new world order and a new reality of being. When we remember where we came from and that we are all united, that each of us brings a profound gift to the table of life, then and only then will we begin the journey to enlightenment. Then and only then will we begin the healing process. Then and only then will we ourselves become the lightbearers and begin to illuminate the darkness. It is a step each of us needs to take in order to achieve enlightenment. It is a step each of us needs to take to preserve the very earth we live upon and to heal the open wounds of our planet.

This is our destiny. This is our mission. This is our hope for a brighter tomorrow.

Chapter 13

UNCONDITIONAL LOVE

"All that we are is the result of what we think.

How then can a man escape being filled with hatred,
if his mind is constantly repeating....He misused me,
he hit me, he defeated me, he robbed me---?

Hatred can never put an end to hatred; hate is
conquered only by love."

\- Buddha -

Throughout life the most profound lessons are learned through adversity. Adversity is one of life's greatest teachers. It teaches us to move through hatred and misunderstanding and out the other side into love and light. It knocks us up against the wall and demands that we move forward. It demands that we look in the mirror of life and see ourselves not only for who we are but also for whom we want to become. It teaches us to move through fear and to acknowledge the beauty of our souls, the beauty of our uniqueness, to stand up tall and strong and to courageously march forward into the unknown.

Each and every one of us is a gift. We are each an integral part of the tapestry of life and we all bring a gift to the table. This gift is as unique as we are and is only ours to give. This gift is the most important thing you can give yourself and the collective whole. It is the glue that literally binds the universe together and holds it into the pattern of life. This gift is the gift of unconditional love given to all of us at first breath by the divine realm. We are all beings of love. We need to love ourselves unconditionally for true self-love has nothing at all to do with ego. True self-love is a journey into humility and it is in this journey that we then find love and compassion for others. How can you know how to give love if you have not experienced love yourself? So the pathway to love is in the experiencing of what it feels like to not be loved; what it feels like to be rejected rather than accepted. Every one of us is on some level yearning for this fulfillment. It is this that we strive for, yearn for, pine for and that all of us have at the very core or being.

We just have to remember who we are. Somewhere along the road of life we have forgotten our roots. We have forgotten we are all beings of love and light. It is through this process, no matter what your believe structure is, no matter what nationality you are or what gender you belong to, that each of us is striving to remember who we are and to be loved. Love has no boundaries. It is a gift of inclusion rather than exclusion. It is in this journey through self that the epiphany arises that we are all a piece of thread in the tapestry of life. We are all part of the whole and each of us is the mirror image of the other. By this mirror image I simply mean each of us is a point of light radiating out of a perfect and unique body. We are all perfect beings of light and are an integral part of the evolution of mankind. It is along this journey of moving from adversity into the knowledge and wisdom of unconditional love that we experience great clarity of spirit and with that clarity a deep awareness and an awakening of spiritual consciousness. When we move into this greater reality of self, who we are will then transform our planet. All of us are at different stages along this journey. Some are in the beginning and are just in the crawling stage; some are seeking their balance and are cautiously walking along their pathway to enlightenment; others are further along and are much more comfortable within their state of being; and some have arrived and have spread their wings and flown. They have truly grasped the need for the embracement of unconditional love that is so needed on our planet. It is said that you crawl until you can walk; you walk until you can run, and you run until you can fly; where you then become one with the light and all that is and all that will ever be. Love has no boundaries. Peace has no boundaries. Mankind creates these boundaries to define his reality. We are in the process of experiencing a great global awakening. We are all one. We are all whole. We are all complete. We are all unique beings that are moving through the illusion of multiplicity to find we are all connected and are all part of the greater whole. It will take all of us no matter where we stand on the road to enlightenment to turn on the light bulb of unconditional love for all of humanity to see and to light the way for all to follow. We are all in dire need of teamwork here! It is important that everyone put down their swords of intolerance, hatred, bigotry, indifference, anger, apathy and ignorance! All negativity is born of these emotions. All of us have at some point along our journey experienced these emotions either directly or indirectly. This is the tool life gives us in order for us to learn and to grow. It is necessary to experience this as it is in the experiencing of the negative that we see and embrace the positive in ourselves as well as in the world in which we live. It is only in the surrender of self that true understanding occurs. We need to embrace our differences and see that these differences are what make us each unique. All of us are capable of such incredible goodness. None of us are flawed. Imperfection is the greatest of illusions. There is beauty in all of life. Look in the mirror and see the beauty of who you are. Embrace it. Honor it and then look around you and do the same for others as well. See the incredible beauty of your world. See the beauty of your fellow human beings. See the incredible kindness, generosity of spirit and the basic integrity of those around you. Look through the eyes of unconditional love at one another and see the hope for humanity.

If you are still confused then hold up the mirror of life to nature; for nature is one of our greatest teachers. Look and observe all of life! Observe how many species of birds, insects, plants and animals there are that all co-exist peacefully together in this dance of life. It is within this dance of life and of balancing our dualities that there is then harmony and oneness within the universe. Pay attention to what is around you and learn from nature. Nature is inclusive not exclusive. Nature teaches us tolerance, unification and a deep understanding of life. Nature shows us great awe-inspiring beauty and teaches us respect for that beauty. She holds a mirror up for us and reflects back to each of us the incredible beauty that is held within ourselves. Nature is our direct connection to God or to whatever your concept of God is. Believe in the power of nature and have a deep respect for her. She is awe-inspiring is she not?

We need to remember where we all came from and travel back to the beginning of our collective memories when we co-created with God and lived in perfect harmony with all that existed in our amazing world. We need to all remember who we are; beings of love and life that were created in Gods image; not the outer image but rather the inner image. We need to learn to co-exist upon our amazing planet with all life forms. We need to accept, honor and love each other unconditionally without the barriers of race, creed and gender. We need to learn tolerance of each other for our differences and to understand it is these very differences that are integral to the wellbeing of the whole. We need to learn to hear and trust our inner voice which in reality is just our internal GPS system, and follow it as it will always lead us to our perfect destination. We need to believe in the basic goodness of humanity despite the pockets of darkness scattered all over the globe. Our world is directly created by the consciousness of everyone who resides within it; the good as well as the ugly. Everything we do as an individual affects the entirety of the whole. There is no separateness, only oneness. We are living within a mutual dream created by the consciousness of everyone. We are all accountable for both the dream as well as the nightmare.

If each and every one of us would send out a beam of light and unconditional love to our global brothers and sisters who are mired in darkness and negativity, the darkest corners of our planet would be illuminated in an instant. The landscape of the world as we know it would be forever changed. Everything occurring now upon our planet is doing so in order to teach us. Even the war-torn areas of the world serve a greater purpose; for they teach us such open wounds need to be healed by us all. The only way conflict will truly cease to exist is when each of us is tired of listening to it. Then and only then will peace have a chance to blossom upon this exquisite planet. This beacon of light will then shine such a light of unconditional love and hope within our world that all of the darkness will simply cease to exist.

There exists in our world so much good, so much hope. It is how we react to the darkness that directly becomes our perception of it. When we collectively see peace rather than war and love rather than hate, we will change the global consciousness to one of love and peace without firing a single shot!

All of us want to be admired and accepted for who we are and for what we believe in no matter what part of the world we live in. We want to be accepted for the beings we are despite the pigments of our skin, our nationalities or our genders. If we are each to have this total acceptance of self then we have to be willing to do the same for others as well. When we begin to see the goodness in all of humanity despite the temper tantrums occurring, we move from the fear of a thing into the embracement and knowledge that we are all of the light. When a child throws a temper tantrum, you gently reprimand them and then embrace them to reinforce they are loved. This then begins to change the behavior pattern of the child from the negative to the positive. You begin to teach through patience, understanding and an unconditional love that you have for that child. You embrace their negative behavior and replace it with positive behavior. So it is that we all learn and are able to stretch our legs and grow. Why then would we do anything less for our fellow human beings who are falsely mired in darkness? Why not take a leap of faith and change your consciousness towards all those areas of the world that are trapped in conflict? What do you have to lose? What are you so afraid of? We are all such incredibly powerful beings who can truly make a difference especially when we collectively move as one united front. When we link one to the other in a common cause for the good of all, miracles will then occur. If we would all send positive thoughts of total unconditional love to these areas of conflict then true healing would begin to take place. We would then begin the process of healing the open sores of the world. We need to believe in the possibility of this and hold it within our hearts. We need to see the world as a living and breathing entity that needs nourishment, soothing, understanding and compassion. When we do we will let our light shine and give a new gift to all of humanity. We will give humanity the gift of hope. Hope for ourselves, hope for each other and hope for our world.

I want to end this chapter with an excerpt from President Mandela's inauguration speech. This speech comes from a man who truly showed us through adversity the best qualities that can exist in mankind. He showed us that standing up for who you are shines a light for all to see and becomes a beacon of hope for all to follow. He showed us that good can overcome evil and that one exists to illuminate the other. This excerpt is as follows:

"Our deepest fear is not that we are inadequate. Our deepest fear is that we are powerful beyond measure. It is our light, not our darkness, that most frightens us. We ask ourselves, who am I to be brilliant, gorgeous, talented and fabulous? Actually, who are you not to be? You are a child of God. Your playing small doesn't serve the world. There's nothing enlightened about shrinking so that other people won't feel insecure around us. We are born to manifest the glory of God that is in us. It's not just some of us; it's in everyone. And as we let our own light shine, we unconsciously give other people permission to do the same."

So shine the light of truth for all to see. Stand tall for who you are, and be proud of the being you have become. Embrace the beauty that resides within yourself and give others permission to do the same. Move through adversity into hope and from hope into the brilliance of unconditional love. In so doing we will begin to erase all the negativity that is enveloping our world and will then collectively bring about a renewal of spirit. Both for ourselves and for this amazing planet we are all lucky enough to live upon.

Deborah Fields

Chapter 14

WHAT DO WE

STAND FOR?

"You can only protect your liberties in this world by protecting the other man's freedom. You can only be free if I am free."

- Clarence Darrow -

The history of the United States of America is steeped in mysticism and spirituality, a mysticism and spirituality that were the backbone of our Constitution and the life force behind the birth of this great nation. We are a country of strong ideals and incredible strengths. This is a nation representing inclusion of all faiths, creeds, genders and nationalities. We are a melting pot of all that is and we collectively represent all that could be. We represent hope and vision and are always looking forward for ways to reinvent ourselves. Change is as much our creed as continuity is our mantra. We embrace both sides of the coin with equal exuberance. This is what America stands for. This is our foundation. This great land has a history of opening its arms to immigrants of all nations and it is that inclusion of all that has given our beautiful country its diversity. The great lady who watches over our nation and guards the entrance to New York Harbor holds the beacon of light that shines the way towards freedom for all. She represents liberty and freedom for those who embrace her. She is the symbol of hope, opportunity and prosperity for those who have come seeking shelter. She is the beacon of light for unlimited possibility.

We as a nation have forgotten what we stand for. We have forgotten where our roots began. We have forgotten that each and every one of us represents generations of immigrants who flocked to our shores seeking shelter with only the hope of a dream and a promise to light the way. It was through this gateway of hope and promise; known as Ellis Island; that many of our ancestors found their way into this amazing country. We are a kaleidoscope of nationalities, religions, belief structures and genders that create a beautiful tapestry. Each of us is a thread in the fabric of life. Each of us represents the continuity of spirit and hope. We have forgotten it is our diversity as a nation that has defined us and along the way we have abdicated our spirituality and inclusiveness as a nation out of fear.

Fear of the unknown, fear of those that are different, fear of change and fear of the lack of abundance are fears like a fungus that festers and grows in the darkest and dampest recesses of our souls. It is a fear embracing exclusion rather than inclusion. It has no place in our heart centers if we are to move forward into a brighter tomorrow. By embracing fear we have come perilously close to losing our soul both as an individual and as a nation.

We need to reexamine ourselves and find out what it is we stand for. We need to remember who we are and embrace ourselves, our differences as well as our similarities and open up the gates of freedom for all men. All men are created equal under the umbrella of the Holy Trinity of love, will and divine wisdom. All men, women and children are points of light in a prism of beautiful colors that radiate from the realm of the divine. When we move into our power from within we are invincible, invulnerable and invisible to all negativity created. The song of the universe sings out in all her glory that all souls are one. She embraces all truths.

She is the infinity, the Alpha and the Omega. She is life everlasting.

We are a nation in tremendous transition. Landscapes that were once familiar have changed and shifted on us. Boundaries that were once recognized and accepted no longer exist. In this time of turmoil we need to extend a helping hand to all who are in need. We are turning towards one another now for comfort and affirmation of being; comfort for what was lost and affirmation for what will be. We are affirming to one another the truths emerging from this vast new landscape will be truths of prosperity, opportunity and abundance for all people.

Our challenges will no longer be those of the past but will now be those of the future. Our challenge as a global community will be to move out of despair into hope and to move out of fear into the promise of a new day. We need to move away from the paradigm of how things were done in the past and into the vision of how they could be done in the future.

We are powerful beyond our wildest imaginations. Our power lies within our heart centers where all hope is born. Within this center of our being everything and anything is possible. Here there are no boundaries, no obstacles, and no limitations. Here within this center of hope and promise lies the vision for our collective future. Here in this sacred center within every cell, atom and molecule the universe sings, vibrates and oscillates to the song of unity. Here the universe sings to all who will listen, "We are one, we are one, we are one. We are one, we are united, and we can never be divided."

We are a nation steeped in diversity and beauty that is beginning the journey back to our roots, back to our beginnings where all hope was born. As we gaze back towards our past we realize how connected we truly are. We realize that every stepping stone along the way has led us to exactly where we are today. Through our lessons we have learned great truths and through our adversities we have gained tremendous strength. When we embrace the negative vibrations of the world we are bathed in negativity. When we embrace the positive vibrations of the world the universe bestows upon us her unlimited abundance and glory. Let us look backwards to our beginnings as a nation so we can truly embrace what it is we stand for and in so doing move forward towards our future. As we journey through time and space within the parameters of our collective history as a nation, let us not forget the divine hand of God created this great nation. It was created as a spiritual blueprint for all nations to follow.

As we move into this vision let us move into the hope and promise of a new tomorrow. Let the lessons and adversities that forged this great nation be our lessons. Let us look back in time and embrace the courage, strength and honor of our Forefathers. The lessons that our Forefathers learned through adversity have made this great nation a strong power to be reckoned with. The lessons we are currently learning are meant to unite us not divide us, for it is only in the unification of spirit that we will take back our power as a nation and begin the healing process.

Over the last eight years we as a nation have been torn apart by events that have damaged our collective psyche. We have been steeped in inner turmoil from the two wars being fought upon foreign soil, the unthinkable and horrific terrorist attacks of 9-11, the economic deterioration we are all currently mired in, by a health care system in bad need of an overhaul and by the colossal failures of Wall Street and Washington which have polluted Main Street.

Many need to go within and take accountability. Many are to be held accountable for the unthinkable failures of these systems. The person who witnesses a crime taking place and does nothing to stop it is just as accountable as the person who committed the crime in the first place.

We as a nation have come to a turning point where the next step we take will define the future for all generations to follow. Our Forefathers laid a strong foundation for all of us. These great men were overwhelmingly Free Masons and as such were part of the oldest and largest worldwide fraternity dedicated to the brotherhood of man under the fatherhood of a supreme being. The birth of our nation was conceived in liberty and dedicated to the proposition that all men were created equal. This philosophy was born out of the turmoil of our birth as a nation in the extraction of ourselves from the tyranny of the British.

With his revolutionary pamphlet "Common Sense" which was penned in 1776, Thomas Paine turned the tide of public opinion and helped give birth to the Declaration of Independence. During this time in our history it was widely accepted and embraced by the masses that the divine hand of God ruled over our great nation and in so doing had established this very nation we call home. Patrick Henry stated, "There is a just God who presides over the destinies of nations". He along with an elite group of men comprised of George Washington, Benjamin Franklin, Paul Revere, Francis Bacon, Alexander Hamilton and John Hancock, just to name a few, deeply believed that a higher power and intelligence had established and directed the course of the American Revolution. They fought for what Roger Williams, the founder of Rhode Island, called "Soul Liberty".

Our nation was founded upon principles of great truths that laid the foundation for national unity in America which became known as the land of the free. As we grew and began to gain power as a nation we had lessons in adversity played out upon the stage of the American Civil War, a stage that enabled us to move into unity and inclusion wherein all men were created equal.

One of the greatest Presidents in our history as a nation was Abraham Lincoln who was elected into office in November of 1860. At that time there were only 34 states in the Union and the southern states had begun to secede fearing among other things, an end to slavery.

In the war that ensued, our spirit as a nation was sorely tested. Many believed the North was victorious because the hand of God had prevailed. On January 1, 1863, President Lincoln signed the 'Emancipation Proclamation' giving freedom to around 4 million human beings held in bondage as slaves in the southern states. A new national spirit was now born. For how could we profess to be the land of the free when so many of our brothers and sisters were held in bondage?

Since that time we have gone through many expansions and contractions of our political philosophies. Each has defined us and moved us forward or has held us back as we evolved as a nation. This evolution of our political body has always been in flux. It has always been in the process of redefining itself.

We are now in the process of going within and asking ourselves, "Who are we? What do we stand for?" The past has been riddled with controversy and upheaval as well as with hope and optimism. We have had many great leaders as well as quite a few mundane ones over the past decades. These leaders have all left their footprints upon the sands of time. These footprints have either moved us forward or have held us back. They have at each moment in time defined who we as a nation were in the process of becoming. Each step taken along this road in history has moved us into the reality of our own creation. Each being who existed in that moment of time and space was a co-creator within that reality. Every being helped define the history of the moment.

Every so often there are leaders who, after having given of themselves in the service of the highest office in the nation, come together for a much higher cause to help uplift humanity. Oftentimes after the completion of a great task greater inspiration occurs. At this time the inspiration to become more than we are is our guiding force. So it was for three of our past Presidents. President's Jimmy Carter, William Jefferson Clinton and George H.W. Bush through their collective work as emissaries of peace in the war torn areas of our planet, have helped to redefine, illuminate and clarify the dream of peace on earth. These courageous men marched forth and offered up their services as citizen diplomats of peace to enlighten the world that we are all one, we are all united and it is in unification of spirit that true peace and harmony will descend upon us. It was through unconditional love, compassion, respect and illumination they were striving to awaken the human spirit in the areas they visited. They tried to bring ideas of unity and inclusion of all rather than exclusionary ideas bearing anger, ignorance and conflict. They offered up the olive branch of peace in the hopes the fists of those it was offered to would unclench enough to grasp the hope of a new tomorrow and of a new direction of peace on earth. They listened compassionately without judgment hoping to intervene and transmute the hatred into hope. They strove to awaken compassion in those whose hearts had hardened out of fear in a collective dream to heal the open wounds of the world. For this courageous service the world owes them its deepest gratitude.

The past decade has been embraced worldwide by leaders who think the unthinkable and speak the unspeakable possibilities of war, terrorism, the use of biological chemical weapons, nuclear war and of catastrophic global climate changes. Out of these negative scenarios has been born an awakening of spirit. Out of this turmoil has come a grassroots movement to move the world forward towards peace, harmony and abundance for all. We have come to understand that each and every one of us is responsible for the conditions our world is currently in and we had better begin to heal the rift created over the past decade.

The administration of President George W. Bush was wrought with unparalleled catastrophic events that no other President in history has had to endure. From the attacks upon our soil on 9-11 that rocked America to its very core, to Enron, to the controversial handling of Hurricane Katrina, to the collapse of our financial markets with two unpopular wars being fought on foreign soil thrown into the mix, the Bush Administration has held up a mirror to us all and reflected back the worst that can happen when we abdicate our power and become apathetic and complacent. This administration has forced us to become accountable and to re-engage in the affairs of our government. The universe showed us in a very real way that what we reap we sow. We are all responsible for the disintegration of the economic, political and moral infrastructure of our country. Whether we had a direct role in the process through apathy and complacency or through the embracement of negative thought patterns, we have all had a part in creating the current situation.

What this has accomplished is that America woke up after a long slumber of apathy and disengagement and began to re-engage in not only the political process but also in the economic crisis which we had all begun to realize was both domestic as well as global. For the first time we saw we were truly all connected. There is a saying, "When America catches a cold the whole world catches pneumonia". It has never been more apparent than now the truth of that statement.

We as a nation need to begin rebuilding the bridges that connect us to our foreign allies. We need to extend the olive branch of peace to all those in need. We need to hold up a mirror as a nation and observe what is reflected back.

We have abdicated our power out of greed, apathy and indifference. The end result of this forced us all to become accountable. We all woke up and realized we were in the middle of a mess that we all needed to help clean up. We need to begin to rebuild our world and to replace confusion, disillusionment, shock and indignation with positive thoughts of hope. This will move our country forward into peace and prosperity. We need to believe in ourselves and begin the journey forward into a brighter future.

All of this negativity has permeated our collective psyche and has left us wondering what course of action to take. There needs to now be a willingness to find meaning in a movement that is far greater than ourselves.

As we contemplate these questions and go within and begin the search for our identities, a new world order is about to begin. We are now moving forward into a new era of accountability and responsibility. This will be both the price and the promise of citizenship. This will be both the price and the promise of freedom. Once again and always the invisible hand of Creation is at work in our world.

For the first time in our collective history we were presented with groundbreaking choices within our political arena. We were given the choice between a woman or an African-American to run for the office of the Presidency. The parameters of our reality were once again redefining themselves.

Our disillusionment with our current government has forced change to blow through the land. Anger has swept the nation and with it has come a strong resolve to no longer accept business as usual. People everywhere stood up in unison, raised their fists and called out for change and reform. People vowed to vote out of office those who they felt were part of the problem and to bring about a new reality for all. This became the season of our discontent! This awakening that is now occurring is gaining momentum and there will be no stopping it. It was clearly seen that the needs of the many were totally eclipsed by the needs and greed of the few. The people stood up and shouted, "Enough is enough!"

Due to this volatility of the issues on hand the two candidates who emerged to run for office seemed to polarize us more than they united us. Anger became the order of the day. If your point of view was different than those around you, the arguments became heated and in some cases brawls ensued. Just to escape the pressure and negativity many declared they were undecided. Never before was there such a polarization of view points. Yet, it was this very polarization that engaged the youth of America to get out and vote. And, vote they did in overwhelmingly large numbers. They stood up, raised their voices and demanded to be heard. As a group they collectively exercised their right to vote and to implement change and in the process they helped change the course of history for our nation.

While both of these candidates that emerged to run for office were good men who each had great values for which they stood, change was in the air. Issues of war that had dominated the campaigns in the beginning took a back seat to issues of economic solvency. While Senator John McCain was certainly very qualified and to be admired for his unswerving service and dedication to this country, for many he was too closely linked to the Bush administration. For that very reason many turned their backs and went in the opposite direction. The need for change seamlessly transitioned into the demand for change.

Every so often there is a moment that defines a generation for all generations to follow and November 4, 2008 was such a night. This was a night where history was redefined for us all. On that night no matter what side of the aisle you stood on, mankind took a giant leap forward in our evolution of spirit. Cosmic forces were at work across time and space and we once again embraced the values of our Forefathers who stated that our country was conceived in liberty and dedicated to the proposition that "all" men were created equal.

Forty-three years after African-Americans were allowed to vote and one hundred and forty-five years after the Emancipation Proclamation was signed into being, we have elected into the highest level of government by a large majority an African American President to represent all Americans. From this point forward the parameters of race will be redefined and shifted into a new philosophy. Children awoke the next morning into a new dream of hope and opportunity not just embraced by some but embraced by all. It has been a long journey into the night where we have evolved in our spiritual evolution enough to embrace the concept that the color of your skin no longer defines who you are as a person.

Hollywood has had a large part in planting the seeds for change and watering those seeds with hope. More recently when Morgan Freeman was cast to portray the President of the United States in the movie "Deep Impact", hope for the possibility of this dream was born. Isn't it interesting that this fine actor's surname contains within it 'free man'. For all men, women and children are free in the eyes of God.

The masses on election night spoke out both as an individual and as a collective whole and our government had better pay attention or those who resist this change sweeping the nation may become as obsolete as the dinosaur. None are exempt. People everywhere will no longer tolerate or accept business as usual.

With his meteoric rise to power from the obscurity of the side lines, a force has been born that has thrown out a lifeline of hope to an entire race of people. This has brought a shattering of the illusion that race and pigment color make any difference in the achievement of your dreams. There is the hope at this moment in time that humanity has now come to a point where we can let go of our fears whispering to us that one person is better than another due to the pigment of their skin. Remember one great truth, 'There are many different races upon this great planet because we have prejudice, not the other way around'. Prejudice is quite simply the language of fear. We need to move out of fear into the hope of a new tomorrow and remember our world is formulated upon the collective consciousness of all people within a kaleidoscope of beautiful colors.

Thomas Jefferson stated, "I like the dreams of the future better than the history of the past". It is our past that has formed us, but it will be our future that will define us. We now need to move out of the past and move forward along our journey of enlightenment and in the process remain present where all great change can then occur.

Our government needs to move into an awareness of being connected to everything and begin to embrace inclusion rather than exclusion. When this occurs an era of honesty and integrity will be the end result of our collective embracement of our enlightenment of spirit. All countries will then have the ability to embrace each other as one brotherhood where peace and tranquility will become the rule of the day. With open arms we need to embrace our allies as well as our enemies and begin the process of healing the open sores within our global community.

The question of "What do we stand for?" now becomes a journey of redefining our parameters and of reclaiming ourselves. It becomes a reality of offering up the olive branch of peace to all people of every nationality, religion, political philosophy and gender. There are no boundaries as to what we can truly achieve. Peace has no boundaries. Unconditional love has no boundaries. We have all created these boundaries out of fear. Let go of the illusion of fear. Let go of the fear of change and move into the possibility and dream of hope. When you do, a light will be born within you illuminating the truth and dispelling the darkness.

Raise your vibrations into the vibration of unconditional love, peace, tranquility and harmony. Hold it there. The reality of the world we once knew has changed and shifted and is in the process of redefining itself. Who will we be when the dust settles? What will we stand for? This new reality is being redefined out of the mutual dream of hope. Hope for a better future, hope for the uplifting of mankind into a higher consciousness, hope for the exchange of peace between all countries and hope for the renewal of our planet.

It has been said the Native American Indians made no decision without first considering how that decision would affect seven generations to follow. Would their decisions leave the world a better place for their children and their children's children? What would that world look like? We should take a leaf from this page in time. I suspect that if every decision made were predicated on how that decision would affect our children and the children of all the generations to follow, the world that we live in would have a very different landscape.

There is a sense of great change taking place. Certainly history is in the process of being redefined. A transition is now occurring; one of governments to be sure but also one of spiritual evolution. We have walked away from old paradigms and are embracing new ones. With this transition of government there is the hope and belief that peace, prosperity and a spiritual awakening will occur for all mankind.

We have elected into power" the new kid on the block" and politics as usual is in the process of being redefined. President Obama was ushered into this presidency on a wave of unprecedented hope and promise that he would be able to galvanize the country and move it in the right direction. His legacy has yet to be defined. The question will now be "will President Obama with no experience whatsoever in either Domestic or International Policies have the vision and the ability to lead America where she need's to go? His challenges will be immense, and it will ultimately be his choices and those of his administration that will define the landscape of America for generations to follow. Only time will tell if he can fill the shoes of expectation held by the collective masses. However, there is the mutual dream that he will begin to lead us out of the negativity of the past and into a brighter future. There is the hope that his campaign promises are those of substance and not just hollow rhetoric perpetuated by his image makers whose sole purpose was to get him elected .There is the collective hope that he will ratchet up the foundation of the ailing housing market and bring us all back from the edge of the abyss. There is the collective vision held by many that through his leadership our failing economy will begin to strengthen and that our dollar will gain its former glory.Finally, there is the hope that he will surround himself with the best and the brightest to facilitate this change and in so doing will leave a positive footprint for all generations to follow.

It is amazing how far we have come. With our choices hope has been born within our global communities that America is once again re-engaging in world affairs and is once again embracing the properties of inclusion. With this historic election many of the communities of the world rejoiced. A new chapter has begun. Where will we go from here?

We have always been a nation who championed the causes of the less fortunate. It is in unity we will heal the wounds that have festered in our nation. It is in inclusion we will advance in our spiritual evolution. One of President Barack Obama's campaign themes was 'Change We Can Believe In'. In this slogan he implores us all to not only believe in his ability to bring about change in our government but he also implores us to believe in our own ability to bring about change within ourselves. He challenges us to move into the hope of a new tomorrow not with blind optimism but with hope that no matter what the obstacles are that we can overcome them. He asks that we have the courage to reach out for that hope, to work for it and to fight for it.

Hope was what motivated a small group of patriots to rise up against a mighty nation but deep spiritual conviction was what insured their victory. English historian and historical philosopher Arnold Toynbee stated, "A civilization in the time of trouble would collapse if its people did not go through the process of spiritualization from within." He also said, "History is a vision of God's creation on the move."

History has written upon the pages of time many examples of civilizations that collapsed during times of turmoil due to a lack of spiritualization from within. The lost continent of Atlantis and the Roman Empire are two examples of civilizations that collapsed due to this process. Who are we to believe we are exempt from this same scenario? If we do not embrace this process of spiritualization from within in this moment of transition and turmoil and realize that what unites us is infinitely stronger than what divides us, our civilization could collapse as well. We should gather comfort from the lessons history has taught us for it is within these lessons we will find the strength and courage to get personally involved in finding solutions to our problems. All we need to do is go within ourselves and activate this power that is the source of all wisdom. There is wisdom stored within each of our heart chakras that knows beyond knowing and will never yield to the structure of linear thinking. It is up to us to free our minds from linear thinking and release ourselves from mental bondage. We do this by being in the now, by being present and in the moment. It is only in so doing that the mind will learn of its power. This power will solve all of the problems we are facing and will find solutions to all of the turmoil we have created.

We all need to embrace hope for the future for ourselves and for our world. We need to never forget to dream. We need to hold our dreams close and breathe life into them. We need to believe in our dreams and to believe our dreams are worthy of unlimited possibilities and to collectively bring about a mutual dream of unification of spirit; a dream that will bring peace and hope to our world. We need to unite as one and begin to heal the open wounds of the world and to never forget we are all connected, we are all one.

Arnold Toynbee said "Civilization is a movement not a condition; it is a voyage, not a harbor". It will be this movement of souls toward a common goal of unity, peace, hope and inclusion that will bring about a synergy of spirit that will then create the necessary matrix to facilitate this spiritualization from within. This movement will ultimately define who we are for all generations to follow and will leave our footprints upon the sands of time.

Deborah Fields

Chapter 15

FREEDOM

"We cannot defend freedom abroad by deserting it at home"

\- Edward R. Murrow -

The freedom of mankind is an intrinsic right that is God-given. All men are free regardless of the color of their skin, the flavor of their nationality or of their gender. The freedom of expression is the vehicle through which we all move into the freedom of being. As citizens of the world the freedoms of speech and of religion are married into our basic rights as human beings in the freedom of choice; not some choices, but all choices. No one has the right to take away another person's right to choose. This basic right to choose defines our spiritual evolution. Within this basic and intrinsic right to free choice we are all united under a global umbrella and unification of spirit.

It is the divine birthright of all men to be free; to be free in body, mind and spirit. The freedom of the mind and of the spirit is just as imperative to the wellness of the whole as is the freedom of the body. When these three bodies are free the emotional body then dances and sings to the song of freedom and soars to the highest recesses of the heavens. The liberation of the body, mind and spirit form the Holy Trinity of freedom itself.

Freedom by definition is the condition of being free and the power to act, speak and think without externally imposed restraints. The freedom of speech honored under our Constitution gives us all the political freedom of speech and action with the absence of interference in the sovereignty of each individual by the use of coercion or aggression from an outside source. Patrick Henry believed in a state of being free and of not being imprisoned or enslaved. In his famous speech on freedom he states, "Is life so dear or peace so sweet as to be purchased at the price of chains and slavery? Forbid it, Almighty God! I know not what course others may take, but as for me, give me liberty, or give me death!"

There is a grassroots movement to bring our nation back to its original splendor in the upholding of the Constitution. Many feel our government has steadily and single-mindedly begun to eradicate from our Constitution the very freedoms our great nation was founded upon. It is imperative that we uphold our vision of a free society where we can all live in a world that encourages diversity and affirms the dignity and rights of every individual who resides within our borders. We are a nation that embraces all faiths, all genders and all nationalities being neither completely religious nor completely secular. That is the beauty of our nation. That is the beauty of our world. That is the beauty of our Constitution.

In the mind's journey to understand and to express itself in the now of the moment, it takes the concept of time which has no boundaries and tries to compress it into time and space. Our sense of self is confined to these boundaries that we have created and have steadily throughout our existence molded into our belief systems. We have adorned our bodies with these very belief systems and have worn them throughout our lives. It is these very belief systems that have in many cases become outdated and in desperate need of updating, both as an individual and as a collective whole. It is our choices throughout our lives that systematically define who we are and who we are in the process of becoming. If the fabric of the belief we are wearing becomes more of a costume related to the past that has become ill fitting and antiquated then why do we still insist upon wearing it? Our beliefs become our identity. Our identity becomes our reality and our reality becomes our world.

Every moment of our lives we have a choice to either accept our beliefs and realities or to deny them and change them. If the beliefs and realities of our nation have become antiquated and ill fitting is it not the sovereign right of all men and women to stand up in unison and demand change? Is this not what the collective masses had hoped to accomplish on November 4, 2008, on election night? President Barack Obama said in one of his speeches that paved the way for this very change, "We've been warned against offering the people of this nation false hope. But in the unlikely story that is America, there has never been anything false about hope." Hope is the ship that is sailing through the waters of adversity to land upon the shores of freedom. Lin Yutang said "Hope is like a road in the country; there was never a road, but when many people walk on it, the road comes into existence." Let us all walk upon this road of hope and bring into existence the very reality that defines all mankind as equal, united and one. Let our choices define us, become us and unite us all in the brotherhood of man, united under the fatherhood of the Divine Source that nourishes us all. We are all one. We are all connected. We are not united because of our diversity but rather are united due to this diversity. It is this diversity that gives us a lesson in unity; that teaches us even though we may look different we are all essentially the same beings of light originating from the same source. Let us all become beacons of light for truth. Never allow yourself to be identified by a label. Truth has no labels. Be present. That is where you need to be in order to come from a point of power and to truly affect great change.

To move into the change that is quickly becoming our reality we must first be willing to relinquish our illusions of the reality we were in. We must be willing to turn in a new direction in order to see the landscape beginning to emerge. Yet, with that change in direction is born within us a fear of the unknown. Marching into the unknown towards the hope of a new tomorrow takes courage of spirit. It takes the hope of something better rather than what we had to galvanize us into movement. We are all marching into the unknown in a procession of spirit towards a new horizon. What will that horizon look like? Will it bring abundance and prosperity? There is the hope that it will and when that hope is held and multiplied by thousands it then creates a chain of spirit that in its collective adhesiveness shines a beacon of light into the world. That chain of hope and spirit is so powerful that in its collectiveness of ideals it is then possible to create a new reality for all. This is a wonderful journey we are on because it is the journey of self-discovery into spirit where spirit merges with matter to sanctify our very existence and matter returns to spirit to unite with all that is.

It is important to remember who we are and what we stand for both individually and as a nation. We need to get back to our roots and examine how we got to the point we are at today. We need to each bear responsibility for whatever our part in this process was and then let it go, release it and move forward. Don't dwell on the past and worry about the future because when you do you forget to be present and being present is where you need to be in order to come from a point of power. When you remain present and are living in the power of now you release yourself from history. You release yourself from the past and from the fear of the unknown. When this is accomplished you move yourself into a place of perfect enlightenment and freedom where you then become a bearer of light in a chain of spirit and hope. It is from this point that you are able to affect great change. All great minds that brought about revolutionary change and groundbreaking ideas and concepts did so from the power of now, by being present in the moment. When you are present in the moment you are present with the universe and great knowledge is then revealed to you. We are all free to be, free to choose and free to create whatever world we want to live in. Imagine the power of that freedom and then invoke it into your lives.

It is our diversity of beliefs that creates the beauty that is the tapestry of life. If we want the freedom to be, the freedom to exercise our political views and the freedom to practice whatever our religious or spiritual beliefs are, then we must give everyone else the freedom to do the same. John F. Kennedy said, "The wave of the future is not the conquest of the world by a single dogmatic creed but the liberation of the diverse energies of free nations and free men." It is our diversity that will ultimately unite us not divide us. Look around you and observe the diversity of your world .Honor it, respect it and you will at the end of the day, give others the right to do the same.

Deborah Fields

Chapter 16

THE CHAIN OF HOPE

"There is no medicine like hope, no incentive so great, and no tonic so powerful as expectation of something better tomorrow."

- Orison Marden -

We are living in a time when we are demanding authenticity in all of life. We are demanding truth and accountability from our government, from our financial institutions and from each other. We are letting go of past ideals and doctrines and are in the process of embracing new ones. Dinah Shore and Winfried Newman said, "There are no hopeless situations, only people who are hopeless about them". We need to move forward into the promise of hope and create a new day. Martin Luther King, Jr. said, "Everything that is done in the world is done by hope". Truer words have never been spoken.

We are living in a world that is all connected. Our community is a global community that needs to unite as one in order to create the changes we all desire. We need to believe in hope, freedom, peace and harmony. In 1971 on a hilltop in Italy, Coca Cola assembled young people from all over the world to bring a message that yes, 'Coke is the real thing'. But the message was also one of global harmony. This message was sent out to the world as young people of all faiths, nationalities and genders held hands and sang in unison the words "....I'd like to buy the world a home and furnish it with love. Grow apple trees and honeybees and snow white turtledoves. I'd like to teach the world to sing in perfect harmony".... Of course they were absolutely trying to sell a product but they were also sending a strong message of peace and unity to us all. These peaceful warriors were a part of a collective group whose message to the world was that we are all one, we are all united and it is only in unity that we will bring peace and harmony to this beautiful planet that we all call home.

These messages that are now being given are not solely confined to the pulpit. Many will come through a variety of sources. Their are many beings who are now working ever diligently towards a peaceful co-existence and abundance for all people. There is enough food on this planet to feed the hungry and more than enough shelter so people do not have to live on the streets. Many organizations have been working tirelessly towards achieving these goals. From your local soup kitchens to your local shelters the needs of the many are being provided for by the generosity of the few. All of us need to get involved to aid and assist as well as to bring awareness to these horrific problems we are facing. We think this is not my problem; this could never happen to me! Yet, it is happening. All over America people are losing their jobs and their homes and many are now being relegated to trying to survive on the streets.

Awareness to the problems we are all facing comes in many forms both directly and indirectly. On a beautiful Sunday morning, May 25, 1986, almost seven million people joined hands to form a human chain of hope that stretched 4, 152 miles from New York City's Battery Park on the west side of Manhattan, to the RMS Queen Mary Pier in Long Beach, California for 'Hands Across America'. It was a very moving and powerful sight. I know because I was there with my dear friend, Debbie, to become a part of that amazing chain of hope. The feeling of harmony and unity on that unbelievably powerful day was profoundly moving.

This human chain of hope, harmony and unification stretched all the way from the Atlantic to the Pacific Oceans. It spanned rivers, hills, deserts and forests. It encompassed people of every race, creed and political preference, the young and the old, the rich and the poor. On that beautiful Sunday morning at that one moment in time, we were all present and united across time and space. We were all one and as a united front we collectively captured the world's imagination by simply standing together hand to hand in a connection of hope to bring about a powerful and profound message. The message being that no one should go hungry and no one should be homeless. We all cried out in unison that we care, that we are aware and that we will all collectively work in whatever manner we can to bring about change. What started as a dream of hope became a reality of hope.

This powerful movement actually began in October of 1985, the year before when U.S.A. for Africa launched 'Hands across America'. This movement was considered, at that time, to be the largest collective effort in community participation and awareness that we had ever had. This collective group of talented musicians raised their amazing voices in unison in order to bring about an awareness of the perils of hunger and of the despair of the homeless.

Since that time in history many other movements were created to propel forward the collective awareness to these problems. Community involvement of any kind is paramount in the fulfillment of this dream of change. We must all get involved and stay engaged in whatever manner works for us. It doesn't have to be huge. It can simply be the commitment to visit those confined to a nursing home and give them companionship, hope and comfort. There are many dreams out there. Choose one. Choose your passion for hope is the vehicle through which passion creates the impossible.

Pope John XXIII stated, "We should not consult our fears but rather we should embrace our hopes". He further stated, "Consult not your fears but your hopes and your dreams. Think not about your frustration, but about your unfulfilled potential. Concern yourself not with what you've tried and failed in, but with what is still possible for you to do".

We have all tried and failed along the pathway of life but the possibilities are endless in what we can achieve, accomplish and create. Never lose hope for even in the darkest of nights the heavens shower us with light in the symphony of stars. Listen to your inner voice as it is your compass in life. This inner voice will lead you down your true path and will cut through all the fears and obstacles in your way. It is important to pay attention to all the signs around you as when you walk your true life path; the synchronicities of life are endless. Life then sends us a road map to guide us forward along our journey towards enlightenment. In ever so gentle and sometimes not so subtle ways, this synchronicity opens up the pathway before us.

When we embrace change and move forward into hope, we leave adversity behind and when we do a whole new horizon suddenly appears before us. This new horizon oftentimes takes our breath away. Hope is a beautiful emotion that opens up the world before us into a brand new vista of excitement and wonder. When we move from adversity through hope, our realities redefine themselves. We create our world every second, moment to moment, through our thoughts and our emotions. This is called 'The Law of Deliberate Creation'. When we know exactly what it is we want, when we can see it, feel it, touch it, smell it and taste it, we then can create it. Within the Law of Deliberate Creation then comes an awareness of consciously creating our realities. It is then our mind connects with the Universal Mind and all things are possible. We are all living within a mutual dream of hope and each of us lives within the parameters of our own dream worlds wherein every one of us is constantly creating our realities every second. Each person's mind is a world unto itself wherein everything and anything is possible. Once we understand this concept completely we are then able to reach out and cleanse, heal and help others along the way. It is up to all of us to light the way. It is up to all of us to show compassion to our fellow brothers and sisters who are caught up in a vicious cycle of despair, depression and hopelessness. We need to form a fellowship of hope and light the way for those who are in need. We need to wake up, open our eyes and truly see the world for how it really is and not for how we perceive it to be.

The world we live in is amazing and vibrant. It is breathtakingly beautiful. It is exquisite. If you don't think so, if all you can see is the negativity, then I challenge you to watch the series called 'Planet Earth'. It will truly open your eyes to the beauty of this awesome planet we are lucky enough to live upon. In a breathtakingly beautiful way, with total clarity and vision, this series brings the beauty of the planet into your living rooms. When one watches this program one cannot help but feel the awe and the splendor that embraces this amazing planet we call home .One cannot help but feel a connection to all of life.

There is beauty everywhere. All one has to do is open their eyes to see it. There is beauty in the smile of a child who is delighted with a new toy. There is beauty in the wrinkled face of an elderly man who is reminiscing on a life well lived. There is beauty in the planting of a tree or a garden that will then nourish an entire species of animals, birds and insects. There is beauty in the building of a home that then fulfills a life long dream. There is beauty in the magnificence of a waterfall that brings us awe and wonder. There is beauty everywhere. One has only to open their eyes to see it, their hearts to feel and embrace it and their minds to believe in it. This beauty that surrounds us soothes our souls. It nourishes us and connects us to God. This beauty is vitally necessary to the wellbeing of us all. Embrace it, become it. It will calm you, nourish you and open up your heart to a direct link to the divine realm. It will open up the window to your soul.

We need to begin the process of honoring and respecting each other and the world in which we live in, for it is only through this process that we will begin the journey to unity. When you honor, respect and love yourself unconditionally you move into a comfort of being and are then able to do the same for others. It is within this process we will each walk our path of authenticity.

We need to do our part in restoring and bringing balance to our world. Mahatma Gandhi said, "Become the change you seek in the world". This pathway has never been and will never be easy but the road that is built upon hopes and dreams and is motivated by courage sees things the way they are and has the vision to move them forward into a new tomorrow.

Never deny someone hope because it may be all they have. Never stop striving for hope. Never stop believing in its amazing power because once you embrace hope and choose that course of action, there is nothing you cannot accomplish. You then move into your point of power and all doorways then open up for you to move through.

I believe the greatest revolution of our generation will be in the collective grasping and comprehension of the Law of Deliberate Creation. When this law is embraced humanity will undergo the greatest of all changes in mind, body and spirit. When we begin to understand and embrace this concept a true revolution of spirit will occur. A revolution that begins with knowing exactly what it is you want to happen and then expands within the parameters of your realities and pushes out all of your boundaries of limited thinking. It is within this process your lives will be forever redefined. When we accomplish this we will awaken to a new earth.

This revolution of spirit will redefine our world and bring us clarity, unity and a collective adhesion of being. This revolution will put to rest old and outdated concepts and redefine them into a brand new vision. A vision wherein we are all living within a collective dream fueled by the power of hope.

We are graphically being shown all over the world exactly how we no longer wish to exist. The terrorists of this generation are holding up a mirror of negativity and hate and are reflecting back the ugliness of these emotions. We are horrified and appalled by the apparently random acts of violence that are occurring before our very eyes. This violence is being brought into the comfort and safety or our living rooms by a media that has united the world and closed the distance in what used to be a far off occurrence. Where we once felt disconnected by time and space we are now realizing it is this very concept of time and space that unites us all. It narrows the playing field. We need to all reject the violence that is being presented to us and embrace unconditional love and hope,

hope for ourselves and hope for humanity. We are all united and held together by our thoughts and emotions. These thoughts and emotions are in constant flux. The universe is expanding and contracting to embrace every single thought and emotion that has ever been created by mankind. All of our emotions and thoughts, both positive and negative, orbit the planet in cohesive bands of thought waves and pure energy that then interact with all other planetary systems in existence.

We can call upon any one of these emotions and bring them into our realities simply by using the Law of Deliberate Creation. When we know what it is we want whether it's the desire for an object or the desire for an emotion and we imagine ourselves having it, we then quite simply create it. We then draw it into our lives and manifest it. The old adage 'be careful what you wish for because your thoughts become your reality' is so true. Envision what it is you truly want. Then test it. Be careful, because if you can envision something casually without much thought and do it with conviction even though it may not be what you truly want, you will manifest it. This is the power you have within you. This is your creative impulse. This is your magic. It is so important to be self-aware and to understand the depth of your ability so that you do not bring a creation into your life without having made the choice to do so, without first totally understanding and then envisioning with conviction what it is you truly want to occur. This is magic. This is alchemy. Once you test this and challenge your preconceptions about what it is you want, very often these preconceptions become misconceptions. The parameters of your self-awareness then expand and your connection to the vibrating ever oscillating consciousness of the universal mind is then absolute. When this happens you begin to see with clarity and then manifest into your life exactly what it is you need. There is then joy in the learning and in the creating.

Whatever we desire and want to bring into our lives already exists within the etheric realm and at any point we can call upon these emotions and manifest them into our lives. For example, when we are searching for the strength and willpower to complete a particular project we can tap into the flow of emotions that have been collectively created by all the individuals who have already accomplished what it is we are striving to do. If you want to be successful, imagine yourself connected to the flow of success that emanates from all the people on the planet who are successful at what they do. Tune into this flow of energy. Feel the connection and become one with it. Feel it permeate your entire being. Imagine being linked hand to hand, heart to heart, soul to soul with this ever expanding source of energy. Imagine being connected to all the human beings who have been successful at what they did. From the writers, musicians, business moguls, architects, doctors, builders to the movers and shakers of the world, all have sent their emotional energy out into the ethers to band together into one continuous flow of thought. This band of energy becomes a global connection that everyone can access at any time. All of the energy you have ever created and imagined exists in the world and has left an indelible mark upon the etheric realm. Whatever you can imagine manifesting in your world will then be created. If you can dream it, you can become it.

We can use our thoughts and emotions to achieve great change in our world. We can do this both individually and collectively to uplift all of humanity. We can also expand our thoughts and emotions past our boundaries of limited thinking towards the war-torn areas of our world to accelerate the healing process and to bring about peace. When we band together in a fellowship of hope, the parameters of our boundaries are redefined and we can achieve what we previously believed was impossible.

When we join together in a collective purpose of love, hope, forgiveness and peace sending these emotions out towards the areas of the world that are so in need of healing; we can achieve an uplifting of spirit and in the process help to heal the open wounds of war. When this occurs we will see an amazing transformation begin to unfold before our very eyes. Tensions will begin to dissipate and the hatred fueling our wars will become absorbed by all of the peaceful and loving emotions being transmitted out of the hearts of all the lightbearers who have joined together in a chain of peace. It is within this chain of peace that wars can be neutralized without firing a single shot. Imagine the truly amazing transformation that would then occur upon our beautiful planet. Within the parameters of the Law of Deliberate Creation the possibilities are endless.

Here is a truth for the ages. "Nothing ever stays the same". All of life is constantly in motion and it is within this matrix of perpetual motion we then have absolute perfection. Every single flower petal, snowflake and blade of grass reflects this absolute perfection. Within this matrix of thought and sound, of light and vibration, of emotion and creation, exists the unconditional love of this ever-expanding intelligence that binds and holds us all together in a perfect harmony of spirit. When we take a quantum leap of faith and have the courage to go within on this greatest journey of all, we come face to face with our own authenticity and become co-creators in life.

So expand your boundaries of limited thinking and go within. Take the journey through Spirit and come out the other side a truly enlightened being of amazing beauty and power. Use that power in a collective chain of hope for the good of all humanity. Become peaceful warriors to help bring about this positive change that is being embraced by so many. Become a link in this global band of energy embracing our planet. Use the Law of Deliberate Creation to change the world into a new and renewed reality for all. Through your thoughts and emotions create a fellowship of peace helping to eradicate war. Have the courage to stand up for what is right, to say no to hatred and ignorance and to do the right thing because it is right. You can create a world of absolute bliss or you can create a world of intolerable suffering. It is always your choice which of these roads you will journey down. Remember anything that you envision will become your reality. So envision the world through the eyes of unconditional love for when you look at the world with love you create miracles that transform time and space. This is the promise of hope over fear. This is the promise of faith, which will overcome doubt. This is the promise of peace, which will overcome war. This is the promise of life everlasting.

Chapter 17

THE POWER OF MAGIC

"The greatest shock in this age of transition...what
you have thought all the time as fairy tales is
actually the way life is."

- Unknown -

Along the journey in our quest for spiritual enlightenment we are presented with the opportunity for great change. If we choose to embrace this change the parameters of our realities begin to shift and redefine themselves and we are left without boundaries in a spiritual landscape that has unlimited possibilities.

Our limited thought process is replaced with unlimited thought and there is then nothing we cannot accomplish. When we push out the boundaries we have created, all of a sudden the parameters of time and space cease to exist and we discover the only boundaries that truly exist are the ones we ourselves have created.

Unlimited consciousness brings us great insight into unconditional love, joy, hope and wisdom. When we move beyond these self-imposed boundaries true magic occurs, a magic that lives within us all. We are capable of so much more than we think. Johann Wolfgang Von Goethe stated, "Magic is believing in yourself, if you can do that you can make anything happen." The Merriam-Webster Online Dictionary states "Magic is an extraordinary power of influence seemingly from a supernatural source." In essence true magic awakens within every man, woman and child when they embrace the unlimited possibilities of hope.

When we move into the holiday season, we move into one of the most magical times of the year. During this season one cannot help but be embraced by the compassion, generosity and goodwill existing in abundance at this moment in time. In the month of December, mankind puts aside their petty differences and moves into a space of inclusion rather than exclusion. We are filled with the spirit of Christmas, Hanukkah, Kwanzaa, the Indian holiday Diwali and the Iranian holiday of Yalda, just to name a few, and in this magical time of year humanity radiates goodwill and unconditional love to all it encounters.

Now more than ever in an economy that has been crippled, we have had to rethink our practice of gift-giving and move back to a place where the spirit of the holidays is more about the exchange of love and goodwill rather than the exchange of expensive store-bought gifts. In the 'Unitarian Universalist Meditations', Victoria Safford writes, "We've already received our presents; ears to hear music, eyes to behold lights, hands to build true peace on earth, and to hold each other tight in love." That is the true meaning of Christmas and the true meaning of whatever holiday you celebrate.

The meltdown of our economy has forced us to remember what the true meaning of Christmas really is. We've had to come up with creative gift giving. We made home-baked goodies and wrapped them in beautiful boxes with festive paper. We made gifts for our friends and loved-ones born out of our ingenuity; baskets filled with items around a central theme, coupons for a home cooked meal and in general just much smaller gifts than usual.

Especially now in our current state of reality where a lot of us are motivated by fear, depression is running rampant. People are disillusioned, their spirits are in disrepair and a lot of them are just downright miserable. Yet, a curious thing happened even through all of this misery and despair; we experienced the light of hope. Hope that our economy will regain its former glory. Hope that our Government will bring prosperity to us all and hope for our future.

During the holiday season people all over the planet sing joyful songs, light Advent wreaths, menorahs and candles to celebrate the light and to celebrate whatever religion they belong to. They celebrate the light to illuminate the darkness and they do so in joy and happiness to honor the holiday season. No matter how dark the darkest of nights becomes, the light will always prevail. We need to reach out through the darkest of nights and embrace the light. There are many things possible during this magical time of year that defies preconceived realities. When we move into the spirit of the mystical month of December, we move into the possibility of magic. Little children embrace this concept wholeheartedly in the hope and excitement of Santa Claus. They are the true reflection of the magic, wonder and hope of Christmas.

When we believe in the possibility of a higher power we too are filled with magic, wonder and hope. When we move into this belief and shed our preconceived ideas by moving beyond our self-imposed boundaries we move into unlimited consciousness and embrace the divine properties of love, light, hope and wisdom. When we do this we are never again the same. We are forever changed and our spirit has metamorphosed with the magic of spiritual alchemy.

Christmas and all the other celebrated holidays are holidays of light and love that dispel the darkness in the long dark days and nights of December and in the process bring hope and joy to us all. It is a time of year that breathes the spirit of the holidays into even the hardest of hearts. A good example of just this is found within the pages of the holiday classic, 'Scrooge' by Charles Dickens. Ebeneezer Scrooge represents the turning away from the light, hope and goodwill of humanity and moving into an embracement of the more negative and darker principles of mankind. Yet, as the story unfolds he also represents the redemption and rebirth born within him as he embraces and begins to understand the true meaning of Christmas. He then puts these principles to work. When Scrooge puts the principles of unconditional love to work he gives birth to the divine properties of hope, compassion, understanding, joy and all are changed.

Human beings are creatures of light. Without this gift we could not have life. When the greatest and most powerful of invocations was given of 'let there be light', 'let there be life' was equally invoked. To ancient civilizations that did not have the luxury of electricity, light was life. Therefore, in December when the days became shorter and the nights became longer, humanity created holidays of light to help celebrate and sanctify all of life.

These holidays of light for the most part centered on the Winter Solstice of December 21. This represented the beginning of winter and from this point forward the days began to lengthen and the light began to replace the darkness. This time of year represented rebirth. It represented life and light because as our ancestors moved out of the dead of winter where all of life seemed to die, they then moved into the promise of spring, renewal and rebirth. They moved out of despair and into hope and their hearts danced with joy in the knowledge that life was once again renewed.

The word solstice is derived from the Latin word 'solstitium' which means 'sol' or 'sun'; and from the word 'stitium' which means 'stoppage'. So in essence the word solstice means standing still sun. To our ancestors there was the very real fear the sun would disappear and all of life would die. So the solstice marked the turning point wherein the darkness was replaced by the light in a renewal of rebirth and hope. This turning point marked the time when the sun returned in all her glory to once again sanctify life. During that moment in history without electricity, the darkness was profound and therefore something very real to fear. Imagine what our world would be like without the wonder of electricity? Imagine how frightened we would all be immersed within a world of total and profound darkness? Only then can we truly grasp the reality of the world in which our ancestors lived. Only then can we truly begin to understand the motivation behind the creation of this celebration of light. During this time period everything in nature seemed to die with the exception of the evergreen tree which came to be revered as a symbol of hope which is celebrated to this day with the Christmas tree. We elaborately decorate and adorn this symbol of hope with lights to represent life everlasting.

Our ancestors decorated the evergreen tree in part to dispel the darkness but also to bring hope and joy to a world which was enveloped in darkness.

During December our ancestors would build bonfires, burn Yule logs and light candles to dispel the darkness and herald in the light. This was done in great celebration with much pomp and circumstance to assure everyone life would remain constant for another day. Due to this, the Solstice became a celebration of light that was as much motivated by fear as by hope. There was the fear as the days grew shorter and the nights became longer that the sun would disappear and death would embrace the land and obliterate all life. The duality of this fear was of course hope, for hope springs eternal. There was also the hope that the sun would return and vanquish the darkness. There was the hope the dawn would awaken with the power of the sun and with it bring everlasting life. This fear entwined with hope merged into a day and night of celebration that we honor in many cultures to this day.

Our ancestors worshipped the sun as a god force and the winter celebrations were about honoring and worshipping the sun as the sun represented rebirth. Isn't it interesting that while the Winter Solstice celebrates and honors the rebirth of the 'sun', the Christmas holiday honors and celebrates the birth of the 'son' of God; a play on words or purely coincidental? I'll leave that for you to decide. However, over 1,600 years ago the Winter Solstice celebration and the celebration of Christmas were merged into one holiday. It's very possible the meaning behind both celebrations merged to become one as well, as the return of the sun represented to all the continuation of life and the birth of the Son of God gave everyone a pathway to follow to insure that each of us would be given everlasting life. Both symbolize rebirth and hope. The leaders of Christianity during that time declared God was the creator of the sun rather than the wildly held pagan concept that the sun itself was a deity. Therefore, December 25 was established as a day of celebration honoring the birth of the Son of God thereby merging the worship of the 'sun god' and the worship of the 'Son of God' into one holiday of love and light. Even to this day one of the pathways to knowing God is through a communion with nature.

We are all creators of the light. The light of creation resides within each of our heart centers and unites us as one. We are all connected. We are united under the umbrella of the Central Sun of God. We are all spokes upon the wheel of life. Each of us is necessary for the continuity of the whole.

There resides within us all a tremendous power that is there for us at our fingertips to be used as needed to alter our realities into whatever we choose to experience. We all have within us magic that we can use to transform our world out of the darkness of ignorance and into the light of hope and renewal.

Kwan Yin in 'The Living Word of Kwan Yin' stated, "Let the magic happen. It's always there. Believe in the highest good.

There is a higher essence to everything. The realm you are in has a heaviness that mutes energy. You can penetrate through it no matter how dark and heavy. Sometimes it has nothing to do with karma. Just don't forget to keep it open. Don't get too bogged down. Don't limit the brightness. Reach through the dark energy and grab it. You might see the smoke coming out of the chimney and you'll even see the smoky sky. You need to reach through the smoke and bring the light to you. Remember the possibilities of something greater than right here. Be willing to go to the lightness. Don't feed off what is not right in the world."

This is what we must all remember to strive for. In our current reality of a broken economy, of a disingenuous government and of wars being fought over the control of religion, land, water, minerals and oil all over the world, we must all remember to reach through the darkness and embrace the light. We must all look through the smoke and see the hope for a better tomorrow. We must all embrace that hope, hold it close to our hearts, imagine it in our minds with conviction and visualize a better world. When we do that we will invoke the Law of Deliberate Creation.

We must all begin to visualize a better world. We must all collectively begin to visualize a stronger and healthier economy. As a collective whole we must visualize a government of the people, by the people and for the people representing all people and embracing all of the values and uniqueness of mankind. The bipartisan bickering of our government needs to be replaced with the inclusion of all ideas, not just the ideas of the few that march to a particular agenda. Conditions that are not working need to be challenged by all of us and fixed without the finger pointing so prevalent in our society today. We need to learn to challenge without condemning. We need to invoke principles of non-opposition and principles of inclusion rather than exclusion to all those who do not share our viewpoints. When we embrace these great principles and incorporate them into our lives, true magic and alchemy will occur and the parameters of our world will be forever changed.

The only way to overcome all of the negativity we are being bombarded with is by becoming aware of being connected to all of life and to each other; by becoming aware we are all spokes upon the wheel in the circle of life, that all of life is precious, every idea is valid and important, and that all actions create equal reactions. All ideas, dreams and thoughts when held with conviction, manifest into reality and we are all responsible for the reality of the world we live in. Each and every one of us can change that reality simply by changing our attitude about it. And finally, unconditional love is the only sword that can cut through the darkness and bring the light to you. With that light brings hope. This is our magic. This is our alchemy. What we dream, imagine and think becomes our world and our destiny.

Miguel Ruiz in his wonderful book 'Mastery of Love' implores us to use these principles. He says, "Let us be aware of our power to create a dream of heaven where everything is possible. Help us to use our imagination to guide the dream of our life, the magic of our creation. Today let something extraordinary happen that will change our life forever; let everything we do and say be an expression of the beauty in our heart, always based on love". When we come from a point of unconditional love there are no barriers, there are no obstacles, there is only magic. Hermann Hesse stated, "You know quite well deep within you that there is only a single magic, a single power, a single salvation, and that is called loving". So let us embrace the power and magic of unconditional love for all and with that embracement let us bring true change and alchemy to our world. Together let us watch in wonder the magical transformation of our realities within the spiritual revolution of the Law of Deliberate Creation. Let us lift up our faces to the sun and feel the light of life permeate our bodies. Let us reach out to the heavens with our gazes fixed to the stars and reach out and touch the face of God. Let us all embrace the properties of hope; hope for a brighter tomorrow, hope for peace on earth, hope for peace in the Middle East, hope for a universal brotherhood and sisterhood that embraces an inclusion of all. And hope for ourselves, that we will find our own yellow brick road that will lead us to our spiritual evolution and self-actualization of being. Find your peace within and embrace it. Find your joy and live it. Find your hope and share it. And find yourself and become it.

Deborah Fields

"Listen to the exhortation of the Dawn!

Look to this Day!

For it is life, the very life of life.

In its brief course lie all the

Verities and realities of your existence.

The bliss of growth,

The glory of action,

The splendor of beauty;

For yesterday is but a dream,

And tomorrow is only a vision;

But today well lived makes

Every yesterday a dream of happiness,

Every tomorrow a vision of hope.

Look well therefore to this day!

Such is the salvation of the dawn!"

- Kalidasa -

GLOSSARY of TERMS

Definitions in the glossary are provided by Dr. Joshua David Stone

ADEPT: An initiate of the Great White Brotherhood of Ascended Masters who has totally and completely transcended the cycles of rebirth and karma and who has mastered the principles and the control of matter and subatomic energy within the parameters of spiritual alchemy. These ascended beings have totally integrated and once again have become one in the presence of God.

AFFIRMATION: When we affirm something we embrace the light of creation or the all present light of the Creator and through invocation of the spoken word through prayer, supplication, and chant or through song we bring the light of creation into our presence and are transcended by it. Through this process we bring positive energy into our lives simply by affirming it. This is an important tool for all to use as what we think and say we create. In other words our thoughts become our realities.

AKASHIC RECORDS: These are often referred to as the Book of Life that has encoded upon the ethers every single person's every thought, word, action and deed from first inception throughout all of time. Simply put these records are God's storehouse of all knowledge. The Akasha is an etheric energy that vibrates to a particular frequency so as to absorb and record all of the impressions of life that are emoted from every single soul.

ALCHEMY: Literally, alchemy is the process of turning base metal into gold. Spiritual alchemy is the process where we transmute all negative thoughts and emotions into the divine light of creation through the process of invoking the properties of the Violet Consuming Flame. Through this process we transmute the negative into the positive and are truly transformed back into the divine light of creation.

ALPHA and OMEGA: The beginning and the end. The ascended twin flames of the Cosmic Ascended Christ Consciousness that holds the balance of the masculine/feminine polarities of God within the Great Central Sun of the Universe.

ANGELS: Beings of love and light who serve the omnipresent God of Creation throughout the vast and infinite cosmos. They are the messengers and heralders of God who represent the feminine and nurturing aspect of God. They are sent to comfort, protect, strengthen, teach, guide, counsel and to warn. Their function is to amplify, accelerate and to concentrate the divine attributes of God on behalf of all creation.

ARCHANGEL: These are the highest rank in the hierarchy of Angels. Each of the seven Rays of Light represented in the color spectrum is presided over by an Archangel who, along with his or her divine complement, embodies the God Consciousness of that Ray and also directs the band of Angels serving in their command on that Ray.

ASCENDED MASTERS: Members of the Great White Brotherhood who are a highly evolved group of beings. They have transcended time and space as well as the cyclical laws of reincarnation. They have totally mastered the divine properties of unconditional love and selflessness and in the process have achieved complete oneness with God in the ascension process. They have through their evolution of spirit, united once again with the Almighty Presence of the "I Am that I Am" and help to guide humanity's evolution of spirit back into the light of creation.

ASCENSION: The process of spiritual evolution back to the Almighty Presence of God or the "I Am that I Am" whereby one has totally attained the Christ/Buddha consciousness through the process of mastering the divine principles of unconditional love, egoless-ness and selflessness in their spiritual evolution. This is the process of fulfilling ones personal blueprint, spiritual mission or contract and divine plan while incarnated on earth whereby the soul now reunites with the spirit of the almighty omnipresent God and the I Am presence of the Central Sun of the universe.

ASTRAL BODY: The astral body is our emotional body and contains within it our emotional field and all of our emotional records.

ASTRAL PLANE: This is the plane that encompasses the earth and is the repository and receptacle of all humanity's collective thoughts, feelings and emotions both on a conscious level as well as on a subconscious and unconscious level. It is a band of frequency orbiting the earth that was originally created to be the amplification of the pure thoughts and feelings of God in man. While these pure thoughts circle, encompass and enfold the earth in a field of white light that all can access, the negative vibratory thoughts of mankind have polluted this field to some extent and it is this polluted field that has reflected back to mankind (who has created it) all of the negative aspects of humanity.

AURA: A multidimensional field of electromagnetic and etheric energy that surrounds and permeates a being or object. It contains within it the thumbprint of unique signature, identity pattern and information of that particular being or object. This multidimensional field has been photographed by Kirlian photography in an enlightening and breathtakingly beautiful way. The aura contains all of our creative energy, thoughts, beliefs and emotions.

AVATAR: An Avatar is a being who is totally self-realized at birth, who does not need to go through the process of spiritual evolution in order to attain self-realization as he or she has crossed over from having achieved the absolute state of perfection of the Universal Christ Consciousness. Having done so, they have descended from the spiritual plane into the material plane for the enlightenment of mankind.

CAUSE AND EFFECT: This is the universal Law of Karma. What you put out you get back in equal proportions. In other words " What you reap is exactly what you sow."

CENTRAL SUN: This is a vortex of spiritual and physical energy that vibrates within every cell, atom and molecule of humanity and all life forms. The Central Sun is the center of the universe, the center of the cosmos and is the point of integration of spirit and matter wherein spirit merges with matter to give life to the universe. Matter then transcends once again to return to spirit. It is the central storehouse of information within the universe and the source of love and light that unifies and guides the consciousness of all life. The Central Sun is the mind of God. The Central Sun is God.

CHAKRAS: Chakra is a term used to denote the centers of light anchored in the etheric body which governs the flow of energy to man's four lower bodies. They are spinning wheels of energy or spiritual centers that are connected with the psycho-spiritual qualities of survival, sexuality, feelings and relationships, personal power, masculine/feminine balance, unconditional love, communication and surrender to God's will, spiritual vision and consciousness development and finally of achieving the ultimate state of being of one with God and God realization.

CHANNELING: This is a process through meditation and prayer of opening up to and listening to a much higher frequency wherein ideas of a much higher source of love and light stream through the consciousness This then flows through you and either vocally or in automatic writing, expresses that which comes through your spiritual channel of communication. It is the process of receiving information through a more right-brain than left-brain method.

CHRIST CONSCIOUSNESS: A state of being that embraces the light of the Cosmic Ascended Christ. This is a state of consciousness of living in unconditional love, joy, bliss, inner peace and a total oneness with God. It is the 'I Am' consciousness that embraces everything in the cosmos and everything in creation. It embraces all genders and all nationalities. It embraces all religions as they are all embraced by the presence of God.

COSMIC ASCENDED CHRIST: Second aspect of the Divine Complement and Trinity of God, Christ and Holy Spirit. The logo, the word; as it is spoken, so it is done. God, Christ and the Holy Spirit represent the sacred flame and also embrace the Mother God/Holy Spirit/Father God Consciousness that resides within every heart chakra or heart center of every living soul; "The I Am that I Am", the Alpha and the Omega, the beginning and the end.

CLAIRAUDIENCE: This is the psychic ability to be able to open ones inner hearing as opposed to ones outer hearing. This is the process through which one can channel the messages from the divine realm. The level that one tunes in is directly dependent upon the development of that individual's consciousness. The more evolved the consciousness, the higher the level or grid that person can connect to.

CLAIRSENTIENCE: This is the psychic ability of inner touch. It is very helpful in the practice of healing and of 'laying on' of hands. Clairsentience is the ability to feel energy with the hands. It is the ability to channel energy from the divine realm for the purpose of healing.

CLAIRVOYANCE: This is the psychic ability dealing with inner seeing as opposed to outer seeing. It is the ability to see beyond the curtain into the realm of the divine and in so doing to see both subtle bodies and auras. This is one of the many gifts one receives when on the spiritual path. There are many levels of clairvoyance. The development of one's consciousness is directly related to the level one will tune into. The more evolved the consciousness the higher the level or grid an individual can tune into and then channel.

CO-CREATOR: We are all sons and daughters of God. To co-create is when one claims their self-mastery and is able to create their own reality while understanding the highest form of creation and self-actualization is in creating with God and the Divine Masters and in realizing that God and the Divine Masters are your co-pilots!

CONSCIOUS MIND: We each have three basic minds. They are the conscious, subconscious and super-conscious. The conscious mind deals with the logical mind. The subconscious functions as our computer and is the storehouse of all our memories, gifts, talents and experiences from our current life as well as all our past lives. The super-conscious is connected to the Universal Mind of God and in reality is our spiritual mind. The goal is to align all three minds so they then function as one.

CONSCIOUSNESS: The aspect of our being that is the direct link to God and the divine realm. We hold within our consciousness the existence of God. Our consciousness is able to split simultaneously into infinite forms and still be integrated and balanced within the whole. The state of being that allows every single soul to be self-conscious and in so doing to realize God consciously.

COSMIC: This is the term used to explain the most universal and multi-universe of Gods infinite universe. It is also used in comparison to planetary energies which are more of earth's focus.

CREATION: Term used to describe God's out-breath, the big bang, or of God's conscious manifestation of the infinite universe at every level, the invocation of God that invoked the light and all of creation in a single moment. This invocation was the primordial beginning of all creation of all life. It was a total implosion of unconditional love, which is a unified frequency that then created the light. In essence it was an implosion of light, sound and unconditional love that simultaneously gave birth to all life. All of creation vibrates and oscillates to the frequency of love.

DEVA: Member of the order of Angelic Beings who serve the forces of Nature and the Elements who assist them to perform their various functions. Angel Devas are the guardians of the forests, rivers and mountains who hold the matrix of the Christ Consciousness to be visualized and held by the souls who reside within a particular area or continent or for a particular race or nationality.

DEITY: A being that is worshipped and regarded as a divine being.

DÉJÀ VU: The process of having the sense you have lived this particular moment before. Usually this is caused in our sleep state whereby we dream this moment in advance and then relive it at a later time.

DUALITY: The yin and the yang or more appropriately, choices we all have at any given moment in any given time frame. Choices that embody the positive/negative aspects for example: superior/inferior, love/hate, light/dark, good/bad, etc. Choices that embody the ever present duality of life.

ELOHIM: One of the Hebrew names for God. The Elohim are the cosmic beings that God created to help Him create the infinite universe. They are the seven powers of God. They are all-knowing, all-encompassing, and omnipresent and carry the highest vibration of the light. They are the seven divine spirits who stand before the throne of God and are aspects of divinity that helped God perform the miracle of creation under the direction of the Holy Trinity.

EARTH: One of 10 billion inhabited planets in our universe with physical life on it.

EMOTIONAL BODY: Dealing with your feelings and desires; one of four bodies. It is our thoughts which create our feelings and emotions so the key to mastering the emotional body is to have control and mastery over our mind.

ENERGY: This is the basic substance that the infinite universe is composed of.

ETERNAL: immortal

ETERNITY: forever

ETHERIC: of or relating to the highest plane of matter in the cosmos; the substance that composes heaven. The etheric frequency and its correspondent plane of consciousness is the repository of the fiery blueprint of the entire physical world.

ETHERIC PLANE: The highest plane in the dimension of matter. The etheric plane is as real and as concrete as the physical plane but can only be experienced through the senses of the soul in a dimension and consciousness beyond the physical awareness of the five senses. The etheric plane wherein the Akashic Records of mankind's entire evolution are registered both collectively and individually. It is the world of Ascended Masters, Archangels, Angels, Elohim and God. It is the plane of reality free of all the negativity of mankind.

EVIL: Extreme manifestation of the negative ego in its most vicious and separated form.

EVOLUTION: The process of spiritual evolution, transformation and change in God's kingdoms that over time slowly but surely realizes the God-self consciously in all things.

EXTRATERRESTRIAL: Any life forms that are not of this earth; referring to intelligent beings that come from other worlds or dimensions.

EXTRATERRESTRIAL BROTHERHOOD OF LIGHT: A grand collective family of extraterrestrial light-bearing beings who serve Christ and the Supreme Creative Force, who come to humanity and the Earth to assist with the evolutionary process. One example of such would be the Arcturians.

FAITH: That spiritual quality that trusts in God and God's laws even though things cannot always be seen with one's physical eyes or with the five senses.

FEAR: opposite of love; the karmic result of projected negative thought patterns.

FOUR LOWER BODIES: The physical body, the emotional body, the mental body and the etheric body.

FREE WILL: The freedom to create your own reality; the option to choose either the right hand or the left hand pathway of spiritual evolution; to choose life or death; to choose either the positive or the negative aspects of life. Free will simply put means we have the freedom of choice wherein we can either accept or reject the divine plan, the laws of God and the opportunity to live in the consciousness of unconditional love.

GOD CONSCIOUSNESS: The consciousness or awareness of your true self as the embodiment in the manifestation of God. The awareness of the 'I Am That I Am' or the I Am Presence; the state of God self-mastery whereby one maintains this God vibration in divine wholeness of the Alpha-Omega principles in the planes of spirit and matter.

GOD: Godhead; God, Christ and the Holy Spirit; three different powers of being that encompass the "I Am That I Am", the Alpha and the Omega, all that is; the Father/Mother God of all creation; Heavenly Father, Deity, Creator and Ruler of the infinite universe; Supreme Being; the Almighty; External Infinite; All Powerful; All Loving; All Knowing; All Seeing; the Supreme Consciousness; the mighty 'I Am' Presence; the Monad; the Higher Self; the soul; the three-fold flame of love, wisdom and will; the Violet Consuming Flame and the cobalt blue flame; able to split consciousness into infinite forms and breathe them out into creation and breathe them back in again; the breath of life.

THE GREAT WHITE BROTHERHOOD/SISTERHOOD: Another name for the spiritual hierarchy of Ascended Masters; a spiritual order of western saints and eastern adepts who have in their ascension of spirit, reunited with the spirit of the living God and who collectively comprise the heavenly hosts. These souls have transcended the cycles of karma and rebirth and have ascended into that higher reality of the etheric realm which is the eternal home of the soul. The Ascended Masters of the Great White Brotherhood are united for the highest purpose of the brotherhood of man under the fatherhood of God; have risen in every age from every single culture and every single religion to inspire creative achievements in education, the arts and sciences, God-government and the abundant life through the economies of all nations. The word "white" refers not to race but to the 'aura' or 'halo' of white light which surrounds them. The brotherhood also includes in its ranks certain unascended Chelas of the *Ascended Masters.* Jesus Christ revealed this heavenly order of saints all "robed in white" to his servant, John, in Revelations.

GUARDIAN ANGEL: Every single person on Earth has a Guardian Angel whether believed in or not. In some cases a soul may have more than one Angel who is assigned to help them. These Angels guide and help us in unseen ways. They never need to be physically noticed and can have a great influence in our lives especially during times of danger. All one has to do to bring them into our live and into our focus is to invoke their presence and to ask for their help.

HALL OF RECORDS: The spiritual location where all the Akashic Records and the storehouse of all knowledge is said to be held.

HOLY SPIRIT: Third aspect of the Holy Trinity; the omnipresence of God; the sacred fire of creation; the breath of life represented by the 'dove'; speaks for the atonement or the at-one-ment of all mankind.

I AM DISCOURSES: A series of books and teachings channeled from the Ascended Masters by Godfre Ray King in the early 20th century.

I AM PRESENCE: This is the individualized Presence of God or Monad within each person; one's true self; that which becomes in their evolution of spirit in the transension and ascension process; the 'I am That I Am' is the God within each of us as the 'I Am That I Am' is God.

I AM THAT I AM: The English translation of the Hebrew name of God as revealed to Moses.

ILLUSION: When a person lets his ego interpret reality rather than the soul or the spiritual attitude system that is innate in all souls then that person is lost in illusion. It is the supreme form of delusion that exists on the mental plane; the only remedy being a soul's intuition and embracement of spirit.

IMAGINATION: This is the right-brain function of the mind which uses imagery rather than thought.

INDIGO: The spiritual meaning of the color indigo is 'intuition'. Indigo identifies a deep source-level connection and holds a focus on it. The meditation upon this color helps to clear up issues of separation. This has often been associated with the Christ Consciousness energy.

INDIGO CHILDREN: These are highly advanced souls who have been incarnating into this world since the turn of the twentieth century. They demonstrate and express truly remarkable spiritual gifts due to their very advanced spiritual nature. They are referred to as Indigo Children due to the indigo color that emanates from their aura. The universe expects a lot from them as they are the ones who will help move the consciousness of the planet forward into the new world order.

INTUITION: This is an inner knowingness that goes beyond logic and emanates from the Buddhic/Christ Consciousness plane of consciousness and the higher mind of God.

INVOCATION: The act of invoking or calling upon a deity, spirit, etc. for aid, protection, inspiration or the like; supplication; any petitioning or supplication for help or aid; a form of prayer; invoking God's presence; a call to God or to beings who have become one with God, i.e., Ascended Masters, Archangels and

Angels; to release power, wisdom and love to all of mankind or to intercede in mankind's behalf.

JESUS THE COSMIC ASCENDED CHRIST: Jesus fulfilled the prophecy of the coming of the Messiah and began the Christian movements and a new dispensation of teachings for the Piscean Age, which was all about love. His life and teachings are documented in a number of scriptures the most well known of course is the Bible. He is an inner plane Ascended Master; one aspect of the trinity. He is the Chohan of the sixth Ray of abstract idealism and devotion which works with the saints and mystics of all religions and is particularly focused on creating unity in all of the world's religions and within all nationalities and races upon the Earth. He is in essence a cosmic teacher.

KARMA: The Law of Cause and Effect; negative energy from past lives as well as the present life that is to be cleansed and transmuted in order to achieve full God-realization. In other words what you put out you get back in equal proportions.

LIGHT: Light is the living energy of God and as the personification of spirit, the light is used synonymously with both God and Christ. The living light is the emanation of the great Central Sun and of the individualized 'I Am' Presence. Light is the source of all life. It encompasses all consciousness, information, expression, energy, awareness, memory, vibration and every aspect of God's love that can be defined through the use of frequency. Scientifically it is defined as a radiation of wave or particle-like forms that scientist's measure as part of the electromagnetic spectrum.

LIGHTBEARER: The lightbearer dispels the darkness and is one who comes bearing the light or one who holds the frequency of light and information for the world. Lightbearer means Christbearer; one who bears the light which is Christ; one who is anointed with the Christ consciousness and bears this enlightenment to all. They are the keepers of the flame whose motto is 'I am my brother's keeper'.

LIGHT BEINGS: These are beings of pure light and consciousness who are one with the Central Sun and core of the universe who thrive upon the continuous flow of energy in the multidimensional universe.

LIGHTWORKER: A being who works for and is associated with the living light of God. They work with the energy of light which has stored within it information and consciousness in all its myriad of expressions.

LORD: The title given to those beings that embody in their essence the Lord God of Hosts, the eternal Mother-Father God.

LOVE: The second Ray energy and the glue that binds the entire universe together; the reflection and essence of God within us. God is love and love is God. The essence of God which is quite simply put, unconditional love that embraces all of humanity in all its forms.

MACROCOSM: derived from Greek which means 'great world'; the larger cosmos, all of creation.

MAN: The manifestation of God; male and female made in the image of God; mankind; the human race; Homo sapiens.

MANTRA: A mystical formula or invocation; a word or formula often in Sanskrit that is recited or sung for the purpose of intensifying the action of the Spirit of God in man; a form of prayer consisting of a word or a group of words that are chanted over and over to become one with God.

MARY, THE MOTHER OF JESUS: The planetary Divine Mother; a brilliant being of great love and light. She is making many etheric/physical appearances all over the world; Queen of Angels; Blessed Mother of Jesus Christ. She serves humanity and the living church from inner levels and works within the hierarchies of Angels and Ascended Masters who comprise the Great White Brotherhood.

MASS CONSCIOUSNESS: The collective consciousness of humanity; the combined thoughts and feelings of every soul on Earth.

MASTER: A title for one who has completed the seven levels of initiation and has become a master of unconditional love and service to others; one who has become a master of reality.

MATTER: The densest known form of energy made up of atoms, protons, electrons, neutrons and quarks, which are the building blocks of all chemicals, minerals and organic forms in the third dimension. Matter comprises the physical bodies of the stars, planets and other celestial bodies that comprise the infinite universe.

MEDITATION: A form of prayer where one, in absolute silence, listens to God; considered the fourth of the fifteen steps to illumination in Eastern Tradition.

MENTAL BODY: The energy field around the physical body that contains all the thoughts you have thought from first inception.

MINERAL KINGDOM: One of the five Kingdoms of God. These Kingdoms are mineral, plant, animal, human and spiritual. This kingdom deals with rocks, crystals and gemstones and so forth. The diamond is the most advanced being in this kingdom. We girls always had that one right! All are in a state of evolution in God's universe including the mineral kingdom. Devas and Elementals live within and among these physical structures and help to create and evolve them.

NADIS: The energy meridians of which there are 144,000. There are 72,000 on each side of the body. These are etheric in nature and are the basis of the science of acupuncture.

NATIVE AMERICANS: These very spiritual people are a race of people in North America that the white man almost obliterated off the face of the earth. Existing tribes now generally lie on reservations that are protected by the U.S. Government. These amazing people practice a form of spirituality that honors and is deeply connected to Mother Earth. They are the true indigenous people of North America.

NATURE SPIRITS: These spirits are part of the Angelic Kingdom that functions to assist Devas by doing the actual work of building the forms that the Devas are guiding and energizing. Through a process of channeling the etheric forces they help to physically construct the plant patterns they receive from the Devas. They in analogy are the physical workers who carry out the architect's blueprints of the Devas.

OMNIPOTENT: all powerful. This is a quality attributed to God.

OMNIPRESENT: all present; able to be everywhere at once; a quality attributed to God.

OMNISCIENT: all knowing; also a quality attributed to God.

PATH OF SPIRITUAL EVOLUTION: The path of initiation where a being pursues the Christ Consciousness and in so doing overcomes step-by-step the limitations of the self in relation to time and space and attains a reunion with reality. In so doing one raises the consciousness, frequency level and moves into total unconditional love through the process of ascension.

PEACE: One of the spiritual qualities that is achieved when one learns to think with the spiritual/Christ/Buddha mind; a state of absolute bliss and harmony.

PERSONAL POWER: The inner power residing within every being that each of us must claim in order to achieve self-mastery and become the creator of our reality.

PHYSICAL BODY: The most dense of the four lower bodies of man. The physical body correlates to the elements of earth and also to the fourth quadrant of matter. It is the vehicle the soul uses in its journey on earth to achieve spiritual enlightenment. It has the potential to be resurrected into the higher forms of the light body through the ascension process.

PROJECTION: This involves using your inner power to creatively visualize your reality through the process of imagination and intention. It is the process of invoking through the spoken word or through thought and imagination the creative visualization process to alter your reality.

QUANTUM PHYSICS: The physics of elementary particles and their interaction with each other.

REINCARNATION: The cycle of death and rebirth that humanity is currently experiencing. This process allows us to continually be born into new physical vehicles or bodies in order to continue the learning process that we all need to move through to achieve spiritual enlightenment. This process of reincarnation is a cycle through which we move to further the evolution of the soul.

SACRED: That which is holy and sanctified.

SAINT: Another word used to describe a God-realized being that walks the earth and has demonstrated his or her Godliness in their daily and mundane life on the earth plane, i.e. Saint Theresa.

SAINT GERMAIN: An Ascended Master, Chohan or Lord of the Seventh Ray of Freedom that deals with ceremonial order and magic which is now being manifested in the dawn of the Aquarian Age. He is the Hierarch of the Aquarian Age and the sponsor of the United States of America. He is the initiator of souls in the science and ritual of alchemy and transmutation through the Violet Consuming Flame by the power of the spoken word, meditation and visualization process. Many know of Saint Germain through a number of well-known physical incarnations such as the prophet Samuel, Saint Joseph, Saint Alban, Merlin, Roger Bacon, Christopher Columbus and Francis Bacon; also known as William Shakespeare just to name a few.

SANSKRIT: Eastern form of writing system; one of the five sacred languages along with Hebrew, Egyptian, Chinese and Tibetan.

SOLSTICE: The longest and shortest day of the year. The winter solstice is the shortest and the summer solstice is the longest. These points represent the two key midpoints between the autumn and spring equinoxes in the earth's elliptical orbit around the sun.

These were worshipped as Holy Days in many of the earth's ancient cultures.

SOUL: God is a spirit and the soul is the living potential of God. The soul's demand for free will and power and its separation from God resulted in its descent to the physical body and the cycles of reincarnation; the subtle quality that all beings manifest that is totally unique and distinguishes one form or element from another.

SOUL TRAVEL (also called ASTRAL TRAVEL): whereby the soul leaves the physical body to travel throughout the universe.

SPIRIT: The individualized aspect of God in the celestial/etherical world that all can communicate with; the masculine polarity of the God-head; the coordinate of matter; the plane of the 'I Am Presence' of perfection; the dwelling place of the Ascended Masters in the kingdom of God. It can also be used to describe discarnate or astral entities.

SPIRITUAL BODY: The fourth and most subtle body in the four-body system; made of pure light that we merge with and integrate during the ascension process.

SPIRITUALITY: soul consciousness; Christ consciousness; Buddha consciousness; the embracement of God; the enlightenment of spirit.

SYNCHRONICITY: being in the right place at the right time; to be in the flow of the divine plan and in perfect harmony with everything. When everything falls perfectly in place and leads you to your perfect destination you are in the synchronicity of life.

THIRD EYE: This is an esoteric term referring to the sixth chakra which corresponds to the pineal gland and sits in the middle of your brow or forehead.

THREE-FOLD FLAME: The three flames of love, wisdom and will that reside within every person's heart chakra and when invoked and balanced connect us to God.

TRANSCEND: to move beyond self imposed boundaries and rise above the negative ego and lower self.

TRANSMUTATION: the alchemy or transformation of physical or metaphysical energy that is negative into positive energy.

UFO'S: unidentified flying objects most often associated with the vehicles of extraterrestrials.

UNCONDITIONAL LOVE: love without conditions, without boundaries, judgments, attitudes, restrictions or preferences.

UNIVERSAL LAWS: The laws of the universe that mankind needs to understand and then apply in order to achieve enlightenment and ascension of being. These laws encompass spiritual, mental, emotional, physical and etheric laws. The entire universe is governed by these laws.

VEDIC: Are the eastern spiritual teachings.

VIOLET CONSUMING FLAME: Seventh Ray aspect of the Holy Spirit; the sacred fire that transmutes the cause, effect, record and memory of sin or negative karma. This is also referred to as the flame of transformation, transmutation, purification, and freedom of forgiveness; associated with the fourth Elohim, Purity and with Saint Germain.

VISUALIZATION: The process of using the imagination to help create your reality. The vehicle through which we must all travel in manifesting abundance.

WHITE LIGHT: The light of God and the Trinity that has very strong protective as well as purity qualities.

WILL: another word for 'personal power' and third aspect of the three-fold flame in conjunction with power.

WISDOM: second aspect of the three-fold flame. The properties of will, power and love must be balanced with spiritual and mental wisdom for ascension of spirit.

YOGA: means "union with God'.

CPSIA information can be obtained
at www.ICGtesting.com
Printed in the USA
BVOW00s2332271016

466222BV00011B/108/P